She
WHO THE Son SETS FREE
IS FREE INDEED

WANDAH MITCHELL PARENTI

Copyright © 2021 by Wandah Mitchell Parenti

All rights reserved. In accordance with the U.S. Copyright Act of 1976, the scanning, uploading, and electronic sharing of any part of this book without the permission of the publisher constitute unlawful piracy and theft of the author's intellectual property. If you would like to use material from the book (other than for review purposes), prior written permission must be obtained by contacting the publisher at admin@iamsherriewalton.com. Reviewers may quote brief passages in reviews.

Walton Publishing House
Houston, Texas
www.waltonpublishinghouse.com
Printed in the United States of America

The advice found within may not be suitable for every individual. This work is purchased with the understanding that neither the author nor the publisher, are held responsible for any results. Neither author nor publisher assumes responsibility for errors, omissions, or contrary interpretations of the subject matter herein. Any perceived disparagement of an individual or organization is a misinterpretation.

Brand and product names mentioned are trademarks that belong solely to their respective owners. Library of Congress Cataloging-in-Publication Data under ISBN: 978-1-953993-03-8

Dedication

She Who The Son Sets Free Is Free Indeed is dedicated to my beautiful, intelligent and unbearably comedic daughter, Iffy Chica. You are my one and only girl, my Shero. You were born strong, both physically and mentally. I don't think that I truly realized just how strong you were until I saw you literally fighting for your life. You fought and won as if your very life depended on it. It was then that I knew I had to continue to fuel that fire inside of you. My prayer is that this book will encourage, empower and equip you with the tools necessary to watch, fight and pray and to live your truth freely in Christ Jesus and to lead as many as you can to freedom in Christ Jesus.

I love you to life my sweet,

Mom

Table of Contents

Foreword	1
Introduction	3
Chapter 1 Fathers And Daughters	7
Chapter 2 The Unthinkable, The Unexpected And The Unexplained	23
Chapter 3 Peek-A-Boo: What's Inside Of You?	39
Chapter 4 Not Good Enough?	53
Chapter 5 When Faced With Infertility	66
Chapter 6 Panic And Anxiety With a Side of Depression	78
Chapter 7 Battlefield Of The Mind	91
Chapter 8 She Who The Son Has Set Free	108

Chapter 9
Daily Prayer **120**

Chapter 10
I AM Who He Says I AM **122**

Chapter 11
Walk It Out Everyday **136**

Chapter 12
Dear God: A Letter From A 40-Year-Old Orphan **150**

Chapter 13
An Attitude Of Gratitude **161**

Acknowledgements **167**

Foreword

A description of this book's author will be as unique as she is herself. Having known Wandah over the past ten years by divine design in the local church, I realize and appreciate more deeply the call of God on every one of us and how He uses particular people to challenge the status quo, confront the boxes that we put God in, and bring reformation to our thinking around who God is as our Father and Redeemer and how He does what He does. Wandah is one of those people and it is my honor to acknowledge her as a forerunner to many whose stories will bring back into focus what God intended when He spoke through John the Beloved in the Revelation when he said,

"And they conquered him (the Devil) completely through the blood of the lamb and the powerful word of his testimony. They triumphed because they did not love and cling to their own lives, even when faced with death." Revelation 12:11 TPT

As a black woman, Wandah is accomplished in natural things like education, professionalism, and all that the world would define as success. However, her acclaim in the Kingdom means much more to her in sharing her life's message.

I pray that you will not only appreciate how God has made Wandah unique through the reading of her story but that you spiritually and humanly engage with her that you might get the full benefit of why she has penned these words and shared her story for the edifying of the Body of Christ, the revealing of the Living Lord to the seeker and above all, giving credit and glory to the One who gave her life and gives profound meaning to her story.

May God bless you as you go on this journey with my sister in Christ.

Minister Leslie K Arroyo Well, CC
Livermore, CA

Introduction

Who am I that you should read my book? Why is my book different from all the others? After all, everyone's an author these days, right? How will my book add value to your life? What qualifies me or what degrees or doctrines do I possess? I am very glad you asked. These are great questions. It will be my esteemed pleasure to answer them all for you.

First, if I may, let me share this with you. Growing up, my mama and I didn't have the best relationship. Perhaps it was because we were so much alike. I never realized it before but it has become so clear to me now, that everything that happened in my life, including our rocky relationship, was never about me. It wasn't meant to destroy me but rather to bring me to a place where I would be able to participate in the building of God's Kingdom.

I thought for years that these awful things were happening to me because of the horrible person I was. I felt that there was nothing that I could do to make things right with God. One day sitting in a group counseling session for post-abortive women, a young woman was sharing a story about the very difficult relationship she had with her mother. There was so much pain between her and her mother. Some of the same feelings and thoughts that she had about their relationship, I, too, had the very same ones. She'd grown so closed, so angry and bitter. At that moment, The Holy Spirit gave me a vision of me and my mama and how our relationship had been once upon a time. He showed me the tears, anger, and resentment. He said, "Share your testimony with her now." At first, I was confused about what exactly I was supposed to share with her but then I opened my mouth and my heart and began sharing my story about me and my mama. I told her how God mended the broken pieces of our messy relationship and years later would use our relationship to heal her relationship with her mother. At that moment, I just knew that this was truly about advancing the Kingdom of God. This was about coming along the side of those who would journey on this same or very similar path and pointing them in the direction of Jesus Christ.

I am someone who felt her life was worthless and unable to be used by God. I am someone who has walked through extreme turmoil. I am someone who, in a crowded room, no one would ever suspect that I was the one in deep mental, physical, and emotional anguish. I was a Christian girl who was having premarital sex, had an abortion, and hid it

for years. I had two stillborn births before I was 20-years-old. I've been divorced twice and I have four baby daddies.

I am also the one who knew there was more to my life than my failures and mistakes. I came to know that God could and would use me and that He had a perfect plan and purpose for my life and I was going to stop at nothing to see His will be done in me. I am not talking to y'all about something I've read about or something that I've heard about. Every word, every story is my life testimony.

We all need a "why" for any and everything that we do. Why did I write this book? Easy! I discovered the recipe for living a truly free life in Jesus Christ. I learned how to let go and let God use me to advance His Kingdom. Your "why" for reading my book is because you want the same thing. Not only do you need to be set free today but you want to bring as many of His children to freedom as you possibly can, right? You like me understand that it's not so much about what we obtain for "ourselves," rather, it's what we do for others.

We can't always control the trials and tribulations that we face in life but we can control how we allow these things to affect us. We can control how we respond to them. This book releases the key that unlocks the door to you being able to control those things that you can control and to be able to respond in the way that God needs you to respond. It unlocks the door that brings you to "The Tree of Life." It introduces you to "choice."

I don't possess anything special. I didn't arrive at this place in my life because of degrees or a fancy job title, or/and not because of any amount of achievements or success. It didn't have anything to do with money, status, or stature. I simply had a burning desire to truly know God for myself. I decided that enough was enough and I was not going to be bound and burdened any longer. I was going to know the God of the Bible and I was going to know His love for me and believe every single **promise that He made to me and I was going to be free**.

Finally, I will say this. This is not an, "I came, I saw and I conquered," kind of book. Friends, I'm still here. I am still living and breathing and the enemy still tries to come for me but as mama says, "I'm on the battlefield for my Lord." The difference now is that I have everything I need to be free. I've got the recipe and all of the ingredients to not only fight back but to win. This life here on earth is not a destination, this is a journey. Take this journey to freedom with me.

Chapter 1

Fathers and Daughters

"Daddy's little girl until you're not. They always say Daddy's your first love, but they never tell you he can also be your first and greatest heartbreak too."
Toni Johnson

Not too long ago I was asked if I remembered who my first true love was. Most of us would probably think of the first boy we kissed or the cutest guy in class who never even once looked in our direction, but, every time we saw him our hair would rise on the back of our necks. I took a moment to think about this question, I mean think about who was my first true love. When I thought long, hard, and honestly about it, I was blown away at the answer but there was no denying it. He was tall, dark, and very handsome. A cliché that never tires, but he was, his smile was infectious and his laughter could fill the biggest of rooms. He was a lot smarter than he ever gave himself credit for. He was clever and just oozed of charm and wit. From the very beginning, he loved his baby girl. Everyone knew it too, especially me. He'd walk through that front door and after being greeted by my grandma with a proper, "Welcome home, Mitch," to which he'd respond, "Hello Mama," he'd head straight in my direction. "Hey Pussycat!" he'd call out and I'd drop whatever it was that I was doing and go running straight into his arms. He was my hero, my protector, and provider, my best friend and buddy. He made my whole world perfect and complete. He was my daddy and he was my first love.

My daddy gave everybody a nickname. I was daddy's Pussycat. I don't know why or where exactly he came up with that nickname but that was the very first of many nicknames that he gave me.

When I was younger, I paid the name no mind, but as I got a bit older, I wasn't so keen on it. To be honest, back then he could have called me just about anything and I would've been just fine with it.

Daddy and I were like two peas in a pod. Mama would always tell us that too. You very seldom would see one of us without the other. I was like Daddy's little shadow, his mini-me. My daddy was a cowboy. He was born down South in Louisiana. He drove big rigs, rode horses, and Harley Davidson's, and I was his lofty sidekick. I'd jump on a horse or a Harley without a second thought and any chance I got to go 18-wheeling with Daddy, I leaped at the opportunity. I feared nothing as long as Daddy was around. I thought he was invincible and so was I for that matter. There was never a dull moment with my daddy. He would almost always be on the road, at least four to five days during the week, but our time together was always so special. It was real quality time. We'd have our fun and lots of it, but my daddy was always teaching me something too. Just in case you are wondering, my mama worked most of the time. That wasn't necessarily a bad thing. Mama was a very strong, smart, and independent woman. When she wasn't working though, she was usually at church or shopping, so I was either home with my grandma or whenever Daddy was home, I'd be with him.

Daddy's goal was to make sure that I was the smartest girl in the whole world and that I would grow up to be a "lady." "You have to be a lady at all times," he would say. Not just any kind of "lady" but the politest, respectful, and most beautiful "lady" ever. As I said previously, every moment was a teachable moment with Daddy. Daddy taught me that education was the best thing I could ever obtain and that no one could ever take my education away from me. He would tell me that he wouldn't always be here and that I needed to be able to do this thing called life on my own someday. Daddy said that knowledge was power and that I had to put education above everything else, except for God, of course.

He taught me about becoming a young woman and how my body and feelings would go through many changes as I grew older. He said that I could always come to him and talk about anything that was on my mind. Some folks thought that he was teaching me a little bit too much. They thought that he was giving me more information than my young mind should be able to handle. In hindsight that certainly may have been the case with some of the things, Daddy would share with me. Sometimes Daddy would talk to me like I was his buddy or something. Just because I was able to understand most things, didn't mean that I needed or should have had access to certain information at that time in my life. He didn't care what anyone else thought though. I was his pride and joy and no one was going to tell him how to raise me. Besides, Daddy had good intentions. He would never do anything to deliberately harm me.

Daddy would always say things to boost my confidence. He was a positive man and an optimist. He'd tell me that things were going to be just fine in the midst of many storms, like when my mama and I weren't seeing eye to eye and that happened quite a bit. He told me things like, "Your mama loves you very much, she just has a hard time expressing it, you can be anything you want to be, you are the best and you are the smartest, you can do it." He was always pushing me to go beyond my expectations. I guess you can say my daddy was my absolute biggest fan. In his eyes, I could do no wrong, or at least I'd better not do any wrong. My daddy had placed me on a very high pedestal. I don't believe that there is anything wrong with a father loving and praising his child, but, I do believe that it becomes dangerous if the foundation is weak due to a lack of a healthy balance and proper perspective. Again, Daddy's intentions were good. He saw perfection in me and required it from me all of the time. As long as I was performing at the level he expected, everything was great, or at least he believed it to be.

If I'm honest this is probably when the anxiety first began in my life. Every day my goal was to be the best at everything no matter what...no pressure there. If you are thinking that's not a bad thing, you'd be correct for the most part. Striving to be the best at all that you do is not a bad thing in and of itself, but there has to be a balance, an element of reality, and, of course, a proper perspective. Children should be encouraged to have a winning spirit and to reach for the stars and yes, to be the best. With that said, we need to know and understand the reality that there may be times when we might just miss the mark and even fall short sometimes. It doesn't mean that we've failed, don't measure up, or that we are less than and it certainly doesn't mean that our parents love us any less. What it does mean is that we are human, plain, and simple, perfectly imperfect.

The Bible says that Jesus was the only perfect person who ever walked this Earth, but my daddy wanted perfection from me and he wanted it all the time, and what Daddy wanted, Daddy got. I could not bear the thought of shattering my daddy's picture-perfect image of his picture-perfect little girl, so he pushed me and I pushed myself even harder.

As I got a little older and got more involved in sports and other activities, my daddy seemed to be working a little more, longer hours, and seemed to be on the road for more days. He wasn't coming home as often. He would only be in town two days out of the week, maybe. I'd still spend quality time with him but just not as much time. He and Mama didn't seem to be spending that much time at all together anymore. I was young but I could feel the tension in the whole house, especially when they both were home. Now I never, ever heard my parents argue but I could certainly sense that neither of them were very happy together anymore.

My grandma moved to California when I was born. She came from St. Louis to California just to take care of little ole' me. We were thick as thieves too. I would worry Grandma to death. I probably asked her a million questions a day. I remember asking Grandma if I can have one of her long beautiful salt and pepper plaits when she died. I didn't know any better, but she had the longest, most beautiful hair I'd ever seen. Would you believe that I slept in the bed with my grandma up until I was 18-years-old? I didn't care that folks would tease me either. Grandma let me travel to lots of places with her and, at home, I would sit and watch Grandma cook for hours. Cooking was Grandma's favorite thing to do. She was the absolute best at it. My grandma would attend every game, recital, talent show, she took me to all of my doctor's appointments and even met with my teachers for parent conferences. Mama and I must have gotten our love for shopping from Grandma 'cause she loved shopping too and I'd be right there with her worrying her to death with, "Grandma, can I have this, can I have that?" She was our entire neighborhood's grandma. All of my friends loved Ms. Moon. Many of the children in the neighborhood would have at least one of their daily meals at our house. They all loved Grandma's cooking. God has such perfect timing though. He brought Grandma and me even closer at exactly the right time. He knew that I was going to need her. God knew exactly what was going to happen next. It does make sense being as though he is God and knows all, right?

My daddy found himself another family about five miles away that he felt he'd be happier with. Well, now those were not his words exactly but they say hindsight is 20/20. I, for one, agree wholeheartedly. What daddy said to me was, "Honey, your mama and I are no longer making each other happy and so would it be okay with you if I moved out?" I will wait for you to process that. Yes, he said exactly that. Did I mention that I was only 13-years-old at the time? I never shall forget thinking to myself, how could I ever deny my father's happiness. I felt that if I said no, I would make him unhappy but that I would no longer be his perfect little girl. I couldn't have that. Of course, I told him yes. And just like that, my daddy had moved in with his new family, with new children, responsibilities, and demands. My daddy was gone.

Access to my daddy became very limited. Daddy

tried to make it work. He ran himself ragged from one house to the other and ran me ragged too. Once I was old enough to drive, I too was going from one house to the other. I had to celebrate two Thanksgivings and two Christmases. I had double celebrations on every holiday. You might think that sounds like fun. Let me tell you, it was not fun. Insanity is a much more suitable description. I was always trying to please two individuals, my daddy and my mama, two entire households. I didn't have time to think about myself or even just be myself. I nearly forgot how to.

I never admitted how truly hurt I was that my daddy left us. I acted and I looked as if everything were great. That's what daddy expected and I believe, at some point, I actually convinced myself that everything was great. I hadn't realized that when my daddy left, my security, my protection and provision, my identity, and my confidence left-right along with him. I was crushed and heartbroken. The love of my life, my first love had left me. Gone. My daddy was gone.

The door closed behind my daddy and another door immediately opened. This door wasn't good at all. In fact, this door led me to undesirable places. This door was the door that led to fear, lack, low self-esteem, rejection, and abandonment. This door opened wide. And so I began searching. What was I searching for you ask? I was looking for anything large enough to fill the huge, gaping hole in my life that once was my daddy. This was such a confusing time for me. Talk about the rug being pulled from beneath your feet. Everything about my life had changed just like that. Not only did my current circumstances change but so did all my hopes, dreams, and plans, as well. I used to trust, believe, and imagine. I used to feel that I could tell my daddy any and everything. Even my security was gone. I couldn't do that anymore. I didn't trust him. I felt as if I never really knew him. Daddy had become, in some ways, just like a stranger to me.

As I entered into my teen years, there was a time when I vowed never to date, never to have a boyfriend. I didn't need one. The truth of the matter was I just didn't want to be hurt again, didn't want the drama that I saw my peers dealing with all the time. I'd had enough drama in my life when my daddy left. One could even argue that before my daddy left, I had a "drama-free" life. My daddy had given me everything I wanted. He took me anywhere I wanted to go. He adored me. He believed in me, but now that he was gone, of course, I started to reconsider things, like dating and having a boyfriend. This wasn't good for anyone, specifically speaking, it wasn't good for me. With my mama and me not having the closest of relationships and her being so busy with work and church all the time, one thing led to the next and I began doing things that I should not have done like having sex.

I didn't even like sex. I mean, what was the point, really? I had no clue. I was just doing anything I could to numb the pain and to try to fill the hole in my heart. I started drinking a bit and partying with my friends. I hated that too. Partying was not for me. Really, I wanted to just give up. The walls started rising. I was hurting and I was very angry. I developed a real, "I don't give a damn" attitude about everything. At one point I thought about leaving school too. I was losing it for sure. I hadn't completely lost my mind, however. I mean, it wasn't like I'd lost my daddy forever. He literally lived only a few miles away. I didn't need to throw my life away. What I needed was to get my life together.

Raised in the Church

I was born and raised Christian, a Baptist. We were in the church at least four days during the week and all day on Sundays. I even attended and graduated from an all-girls Catholic school. I had my fair share of religion regularly. I was not lacking in the good morals and values department, but at that time, I was wounded and conflicted. Reflecting, my life, my entire identity had been wrapped up in my daddy and my daddy had left me. He broke the promises he made to me and he removed his covering from me, his provision, too.

Daddy's love was wonderful until it was gone. It

turns out his love was conditional and self-serving. His love was quite limited. So keeping to my Christian upbringing, after Daddy left, I went to church all the time and prayed and prayed from God to take the pain away. I sang in the choir and even went to Sunday School. I did everything I could think of to relieve the pain I felt. Nothing seemed to work, but, you see, I just kept going to church. I kept singing, and Lord knows that I kept praying. I would not, could not, and did not stop.

Now, I knew that God was real. Our relationship had started back when I was just eight-years-old. He put something down on the inside of me the day that I was baptized. It was like fire or something and I believed that He really was with me and that the pain would finally go away. For some reason now though, I felt that maybe He'd left me too. After all, my first love, my own daddy had left me.

Do you see what happened? My first love and the pain and disappointment that ensued had set the tone for how I'd approach and view every relationship that would come next in my life. The Bible says seek and ye shall find, so I sought hard for my God but lacked the faith and confidence to believe that He'd show Himself to me. Would He want me or perhaps, He would no longer be with me? I began to think that just as Daddy left me, God had left me as well. I'd heard the preacher say things like, "Jesus would never leave nor forsake you," but in my mind Daddy did, so why wouldn't Jesus? The Bible also says, "The devil is a liar, the father of lies." I must say that is something that I now believe. Still, I felt like I wasn't seeing God for who He truly was.

What I read and what I was being taught in church was very contradictory. It just didn't make sense to me, so I changed churches. I left the church that I'd grown up in all my life. This was major, like something you just don't do, ever. My mama was angry with me. I left aunties, cousins, and everybody. I think that she was kind of embarrassed more than anything but I was on a real mission. I was seeking my God at all cost and I was going to find Him and He was going to love me, (in my Jennifer Holiday voice).

That time in my life was what I now lovingly consider to be my, "humbling beginnings." I learned a lot about prioritizing. It's funny because my daddy used to always say to me, "Puss, don't put the cart before the horse." This basically meant that I needed to prioritize and put first things first. A cart cannot pull horses. The same goes for what we teach and instill in our children, right? The first love a child should learn about is the love of their Heavenly Father because that will give them a firm foundation, upon this every other relationship and love will be built. Even when the enemy rushes in to attempt to kill, steal, and destroy, they will never be able to penetrate that firm foundation built on their Heavenly Father and His Love for them.

Growing up, my cart was trying to pull the horses. God was not the priority. He was not put first. Even though I was raised in a Christian home and attended church on the regular, I saw God the same way I saw my daddy. My foundation had been built on man or you might say sand. It was weak. It could just wash away and that's exactly what happened. But, God doesn't wash away or go away. He really doesn't leave or forsake you and when I believed at eight-years-old that he was with me, He was and He'd never left me. I was looking high and low searching for God but He'd never even left. Because from the beginning I'd only learned the love of man, my daddy, and not the love of my Heavenly Father, my approach to every other relationship would ultimately look like the first.

I was a grown-up woman before I came to really know God for the God that He really and truly is and be able to accept and embrace His love for me as His daughter. Psalms 139:13 reads, "For you created my inmost being; you knit me together in my mother's womb." From the very beginning of my life, because He created me, He's been right there. 1 John 4:8 says, "He that loveth not knoweth not God; for God is love." God is the very essence of love. Not the kind of love that we see from man. This is a Godly love that we have never known. I Corinthians 13 describes it this way and let us change the word love to God since God is love, "God is patient, God is kind, He does not envy, He does not boast, God is not proud. God is not rude, God is not self-seeking, God is not easily angered, God keeps no record of wrongs. God does not delight in evil but He rejoices with the truth. God always protects, always trusts, always hopes, and always preserves. God never fails." Knowing and understanding those words is a total game-changer, at least it has been for me.

Our approach to God cannot be the same as our approach to man. Otherwise, we will always be searching for something that has always been with us but we just didn't know exactly how to access Him. Also, we would have the same expectations from God as we do from man. This means that we would never really know Him or trust Him but, as a good friend of mine once told me, "When you know better, you do better?" I'm choosing to do better.

Chapter Reflection:

"My heart was broken and my soul crushed early in life. I was an innocent child hurt by someone in whom I'd put my trust."

Read and Meditate:

    Matthew 19:14

    Matthew 18:10

    Ephesians 6:4

    Mark 10:14

Chapter 2

The Unthinkable, the Unexpected and the Unexplained

"Life isn't always what we've planned but when we are called we need to lead. The calling might leave you feeling broken, but the fight will transform you and the change you create will allow you to heal."
Taun Hall

Have you ever heard of a "Self-Proclaimed Prophecy?" Well, a Self-Proclaimed Prophecy by definition is a socio psych-ological phenomenon of someone "pre-dicting" or expecting something, and this prediction or expectation comes true simply because one believes it will, and their resulting behaviors align to fulfill those beliefs. That would not be the case with me at all in this story.

Oh, I tried to predict my future. I think that some of us may be guilty of this and God says, "That's so sweet, it's really cute," and then He smiles and says, "And yet here are my plans for your life." Oddly enough, His plans may not be so different from what we were predicting, however, God may have a completely different road map for how we will arrive at our intended destination.

Contrary to what I thought I wanted, I actually had a boyfriend in the latter part of high school but still, no one believed that I would ever get married or have children. I'm not exactly certain why that was, but at least those who believed that were pretty spot on. I had no intention of ever getting married or having any children. In fact, I'm pretty sure that I said that out loud more than a few times. And even though I had a steady boyfriend at the time, I truly only dreamed of wanting to be the tiniest, most petite runway model in the whole world. My mother sent me to modeling school and I had an agent who told me that at only 5" height I could do it. He said that I could go to Japan and be successful, and I was ready. I floated effortlessly down the runway as if I were as tall as any of the high fashion models in Paris. My catwalk was the cat's meow for sure. My ultimate dream was life in fashion and I could not see how a husband and children were going to fit into that picture.

I'd done a pretty good job of dodging the whole "boyfriend" thing. Don't get me wrong. I flirted a lot. I had my share of crushes, but being in a serious relationship with one guy, was really not something that I was interested in. Many of my friends had boyfriends and there was always some kind of drama and I don't do drama. You know that ole' saying? "Save the drama for yo mama!" And since, at the time I was nobody's mama, I wasn't having any drama. But that would all change soon enough and we'll eventually get to that part. Let's just stay focused here. I was determined to stay in the "single ladies" lane and I was quite happy with that. No-fuss, no muss, and the best part of all, no drama.

So here's how it all went down. One of my closest friends said to me one day, "I have the perfect guy for you."

I replied, "Honey those are fighting words and what exactly do you mean by perfect?"

She said that she thought this guy was perfect for me because we both were models, into fashion, smart, etc. and he was cool and super cute. "Well, sign me up then," I replied jokingly. I was not budging on my decision to not have a steady boyfriend but then she showed me a picture of him and I found myself giving him my phone number. I could not believe it. Seriously, that young man was fine. He was one of those Creole boys. Creole was very much in style back then. If you had a good looking Creole guy by your side, you were the envy of many. I thought he was the most beautiful boy I'd ever seen, like ever. My best friend also thought he was gorgeous and felt the need to let him know how she was feeling but he chose me. Truth be told, I liked being chosen by him, I liked all of the attention but I'm not sure I truly was ready to give myself over to being in a serious committed relationship. It wasn't just that I didn't want any drama. I was afraid of being hurt.

Now I know that this may sound crazy but I suppose what I'm really trying to say is, I didn't want to put all my eggs in one basket only to have someone come along and take my entire basket, eggs and all breaking my heart just like my daddy had done. I think this is what they mean by, "damaged goods." My daddy had left me a little damaged. It was very hard for me to trust anyone. My boyfriend was literally no better off than I was. He'd also been pretty hurt by both of his parents growing up. They'd left him at his grandparent's home for them to raise and did not return for him. Let's just say we'd become quite the pair, unable to trust each other, totally and completely insecure, very broken but we gave it a go anyhow.

We dated for a year, got engaged in the second year, and married five months after I graduated from high school. Yes, I said I wasn't doing it, but I'll say it again, he was fine, Creole fine. Need I say more?

Have you ever sung this song growing up, "First comes love, then comes marriage and then comes Suzy with a baby carriage?" That was me, the girl who absolutely did not want anything to do with getting married or having children. Obviously, that whole idea went right out of the window. There was love and marriage and eventually, there would be a baby carriage.

Imagine with me if you will. You are in the most serious relationship of your life at the very young age of eighteen-years-old and to that end, you are about to get married. That's right, married at eighteen-years-old. Now you have just started college and are trying to figure out what exactly it is you'd like to do with your life. Keep tracking with me. Let's add the fact that you are now also pregnant. No, that is not a typo – Pregnant!

If you are already thinking that's a lot, you are absolutely right. It wasn't something that was considered common but it was indeed happening to me all at once. It was a lot. Aside from morning sickness and this thing where I could not swallow my own spit so I was constantly spitting, I had a great pregnancy, or so I thought. I never missed my doctor's appointments. I was never a terrible eater or an overeater. I had no trips, slips, nothing unusual or harmful happened during my pregnancy. There was not a single warning sign that something was ever going wrong but, the morning of my due date, I woke up with a bit of headache, nothing major or uncommon when you are nine months pregnant.

I prepared for my routine doctor's appointment that my mama drove me to. Everything was status quo. I weighed in, I gave my usual urine sample, the nurse took my blood pressure, I got undressed and waited for my doctor to come and listen to the baby's heartbeat as per usual. I loved my doctor. Dr. Gordon treated me just like I was his own daughter, not like another number. He never made me feel bad or uncomfortable because I was a pregnant teenager. He was a very kind, caring, and gentle physician. You could tell he really loved what he did. He would make me feel calm with his great sense of humor and he was one of the sharpest dressers ever. You could definitely say that his fashion game was on point for sure. He walked into the room and we celebrated the fact that it was our due date and then he sat down to listen to the baby's heartbeat.

All of sudden, Dr. Gordon's usual smile turned completely upside down. He looked very concerned. I asked if everything was okay and he told my mom to take me immediately to the specialist for an emergency ultrasound. He said the baby's heartbeat was quite faint.

The ultrasound doctor was at least ten minutes away with no traffic. We arrived in less than seven minutes. The doctor was waiting for us and had everything in place. I laid on the examination table and he hooked me up to the fetal monitor to hear the heartbeat and there was also a screen so we could see if the baby had any problems. Unfortunately, for me, again the doctor had that same concerned, worried look on his face that Dr. Gordon had and then he said the words, "I cannot find a heartbeat." I thought there must be some mistake. I said, "Mama, I don't understand. Do something!"

I was so scared. I was confused. The ultrasound doctor told my mom to take me to the hospital immediately. He would let them know that we were coming. Strangely enough, he also told us that I was in labor and we needed to hurry. I don't remember much about the ride to the hospital, only that we got there safely and very quickly. Much of that day is a blur to me but I do know that it would later prove to be one of the most memorable experiences of my life. Once we were there in the hospital, I was given the exact testing all over again, and again there was **no heartbeat**. My baby had died. There was such a rush of emotions. It was like having the worst nightmare imaginable but you are wide awake. You can't change it nor stop it. I began thinking the most awful thoughts. I could not believe what was happening to me and why it was happening to me. What did I do to ever deserve such a horrific fate? Was it the "Dead Baby Joke Book" I had read a few years prior? Someone brought this horrible book to our school and my friends and I read it and laughed at those terrible, terrible jokes. *We were just young, silly, and we really didn't mean any harm...but could that be why God had taken my baby?* I'd thought. "Why is God doing this to me? I am a good girl...why?" I asked my mama. She quickly rebuked me and said,

'Child, don't you ever question God.' She told me that I only needed to trust Him and that, in time, He'd show me why He had chosen to take His child back home. I was in too much pain for any further discussion with her on the subject so I just said, "Okay Mama."

I lay in my hospital bed on that 13th day in April 1986, agonizing and laboring in childbirth, trying to deliver my baby that I knew was no longer with us and who wouldn't be going home with me. Thankfully, my dear friends were there in the hospital praying and laboring right along with me. True friends are more precious than gold. If you are lucky to have one in your lifetime, consider yourself a very rich individual. A true friend is priceless. I've been lucky to have more than a few. It was unbelievable.

When I was growing up, mostly, if you got pregnant at a young age as I had, you were mocked and usually, no one wanted anything to do with you. You were usually sent away in secret before anyone knew you were pregnant. You'd have your baby and often the child would be put up for adoption. When you returned no one would even know of the incident. That was not the case for me. I stayed right at home surrounded by my family and my friends. My daddy said he'd never seen so many little girls with so many tears for anyone at the hospital that evening. As much as I was in pain and wanting to just give up, they were my saving grace. I don't remember if I ever told them that but it's true and I'll always love them for that. Again, so much of that day is missing but my little angels being there for me I won't ever forget.

After hours of major pain and just about the time that I was ready to give up the ghost, I mean just throw in the towel, and oh yes, by the way, whoever said that labor doesn't hurt is not being truthful with us at all, not only does it hurt, it hurts really bad. All of a sudden I felt God's presence all around me. My mama was right next to me, holding my hand with her left hand and her Bible with her right hand. In an instant, I went from not being close to being ready to deliver, to pushing and then meeting the most beautiful baby boy in the whole world.

I tell you that I saw the hand of God move mightily and swiftly in those few moments. It was incredible but indescribable all at the same time. All I can say is that it was certainly God. What should have rocked my faith to its very core actually sealed it. If I had any doubt before about my faith or God, there wasn't any doubt anymore. God moved in and through me, I gave birth to baby Adam. He was my first stillborn baby, my sweet, sleeping angel.

What would come next? I wondered. I do remember that this was one of the most painful experiences for me, ever. The nurse placed the baby Adam on my chest for a brief moment. I'm not really sure why she did because it was almost unbearable at that time. In hindsight though, I'm glad that she did. I'm sure that I would have regretted not holding my son if she had not.

Shortly after, I could feel myself starting to slip in and out of reality. They said that it was the shock of it all. My father was taking pictures of me and the baby which I know seemed odd but that was just my daddy's way. I'm told that folks from the south did that sort of thing and Daddy was just country, plain and simple.

Later on, I was wheeled into my room and everyone had gone for the evening. In the room, there was no one there except for me and a nurse. The room was white, sterile, empty, and ever so cold. The nurse was giving me an IV and I could remember tasting alcohol in my throat. She was talking but her voice kept getting further and further away from me. Soon I heard nothing. I saw nothing. I felt nothing except nothing. Some days later I was released from the hospital. That must have been the day I finally came back to myself because I don't remember anything in between. Daddy had picked me up from the hospital, and on the ride home, there was this overwhelming feeling of grief, sadness, and emptiness. This was yet another loss for me. First, there was my daddy when he left us and now my beautiful baby boy. The hole in my heart just grew bigger and bigger. *Would I ever be able to fill it again,* I wondered?

Let me tell you one thing. Never, never ask the question, "what's next?" Next for me would be another unexpected pregnancy just a few months later which preceded an unthinkable and unimaginable second stillborn birth. This time around it was my daughter, Sariah, my real life in

Dejà Vu. I didn't dream of it. I was awake and actually living it. By then I was really thinking, what is wrong with me? I'm barely 20-years-old. This isn't normal. I must be broken, definitely cursed, or something. I decided that God just did not like me. I convinced myself of it. My doctors had run so many tests trying to figure out if there was some underlying illness or if there was something I needed that my body was deficient in. All tests came back negative and clear. I was perfectly healthy. It didn't make sense though and it didn't change the fact that I felt inadequate and imperfect. I felt like a failure, my body was broken and my soul and spirit were crushed. I was damaged goods.

These were very hard and dark times for me, although no one would know it to look at me. No one would ever have guessed it but I was hanging on by a thread. Every day was a struggle. I had fallen into that deep black hole and I couldn't seem to dig my way out of it. I don't even know if I ever really tried. I felt at times as if I were screaming for help. Help me! It seemed like no one could hear me. I didn't just lose my babies. I lost myself as well.

I threw myself into my modeling. When I was on the runway, I was no longer that sad person. I became whatever I was wearing. If it were a sportswear scene, I'd become a famous athlete, a champion. If it was evening wear, I became the most beautiful belle at the ball. Modeling was my escape.

I could be anyone I wanted to be on that runway.

Consequently, it was doing more harm than good. Not only was the escaping only for brief moments, but they also weren't real. My agent would always coach me to lose five more pounds. I only weighed 86 lbs. at the time so on top of everything, I'd developed an eating disorder. I was sinking, sinking deeper and deeper into the black hole. I told you. Never, never ask the question, "what's next?" Trust and believe you may not like it and almost will never be prepared for it.

Though I believed that God didn't like me at that particular time in my life, He was all that I had and I loved Him. Maybe this was payback for my disobedience, having premarital sex, laughing at dead baby jokes, and not being especially nice to my mother all of the time. Maybe it was because of some of the things that I harbored in my heart against others or some of the other things I'd done that were not exactly the most Christian things to do. I wasn't sure but I was going to do better, be a better person so that He would hear my cries, answer my prayers and hopefully love me again and not let these awful things continue to happen to me. I prayed daily. I prayed without ceasing. That was one of the greatest gifts, besides teaching me about Jesus that my mama had given me. Mama was a praying woman. I'd seen her on her knees crying out to The Lord early in the morning before the sun came up as well as before she went to bed at night. She taught me to do the same. Prayer became my lifestyle. I prayed and had conversations with The Lord all day long, every day. It was not just an event or ritual for me. It was like breathing. It worked too.

On December 16th the following year, God blessed my then-husband and me with a beautiful, healthy baby boy, a son, a junior. God is good all the time. Mama was right as she was most times. Those moments taught me; you don't ever need to question God. You need only to trust Him. In time, He will show you or tell you why He allows things. Now He may not always give you all of the answers but that's okay too. Proverbs 3:5-6 tells us to, "Trust in The Lord with all thine heart; and lean not unto thine own understanding. In all thy ways acknowledge Him, and He shall direct thy paths." I love that it first tells me to trust The Lord and then it tells me to not try and figure things out on my own. It releases me of the burden of trying to figure it myself. It makes me feel like God's got me in all things. I'd also like to share that His ways are neither our ways nor His thoughts our thoughts. I like that because He's God, they aren't supposed to be, right? But we can find solace in that Jeremiah 29:11 says this, "For I know the thoughts that I think toward you, saith The Lord, thoughts of peace and not of evil, to give you an expected end." So whereas some things in this life might be unthinkable, unexpected, and unexplained, we can rest assured that our God will give us an expected end. In the end, we all win in Christ Jesus. He gave me double for my trouble. I lost two children, yes but today I am the mother of four beautiful children and six grandchildren.

Won't He Do It!

Chapter Reflection:

"When making plans for our lives we must keep in mind that our lives are not our own. We belong to God and He has plans of His own. Only trust Him."

Read and Meditate:

    Jeremiah 29:11

    Proverbs 19:21

    Isaiah 14:24

    John 14:27

Chapter 3

Peek-a-Boo: What's Inside Of You?

"Knowing yourself is learning to love yourself enough to give and receive true and lasting love."
Lynn Jackson

So what's your type? Do you have one? Most of us do. Do you prefer the tall dark and handsome or the light-skinned with pretty eyes and good hair? Back in my high school days, I remember we called ourselves having, "a type." My type has since changed but back then. I was into the "pretty boys." I know that it sounds ridiculous and truly it was but I loved some tall light-skinned brothers with pretty eyes and good hair. I didn't mind the color so much. For me, it was about the long eyelashes and I loved the basketball players with those long, lanky legs. A pretty smile with dimples was just the icing on the cake, okay. Some of my sister-girlfriends liked the tall, dark, and handsome type, others liked the muscles, the bad boy type. Having these so-called types, looking back, was one of the silliest things ever. We used to say things like, "When I grow up my husband is going to be 'fine'." That was honestly one of the most important characteristics back then. If I'm honest, even today, some women that I've spoken to on this matter, still have this as the number one item on their list when looking for romance. The man has to be "fine."

I told you my story earlier about meeting my first husband in high school through a sister-girlfriend of mine. Yes, you read it correctly, my "first husband." Don't judge me. Anyway, he was one of those, "fine" types. He had long jet-black, straight hair like an Indian. His eyes were nice and he had a

PEEK-A-BOO: WHAT'S INSIDE OF YOU?

beautiful smile. He had cinnamon-brown skin, not exactly light-skinned but that was okay. We'll just put a pin in that and come back to that in just a bit. Also, take note that there were a few characteristics I initially mentioned that ultimately were not present. Anyway, he was probably still one of the most beautiful individuals that I'd ever seen in my life. He was smart, funny sometimes but, as far as us being compatible and having similar interests, values, standards, hopes, dreams, etc. those things I never even considered. None of that seemed to matter.

I was wrong because it did matter. It all mattered. My focus was purely based on the image. What he looked like and how we looked together as a couple was my focus. How others saw us, for some reason, mattered more than anything else, or so I thought. I was wrong. We were all wrong. Getting to know who someone really is very important. What does he/she want in life, what do they like/dislike, do they believe in God, what are their thoughts about having children, what are their political views, would they feed the homeless, do they have a good relationship with their mother/father, what are their plans related to work? All of these questions and so many more matter. It's the difference between having a happy, loving, and meaningful relationship and having a miserable one. Not that one of you is better than the other but you could really just be incompatible, not a good match for one another. You could be perfectly perfect for someone else, just not each other. Let's just say that happened to me.

We could actually say that's happened to me a few times. Yes, there I've said it. I've skied down that slippery slope a few times. The question is why? Why did I continue to make the same choices for the same reasons? I remember being so unhappy to the point of becoming ill, and so I went to see Dr. Gordon to confess my woes and he said to me, "You know you married the same person twice?" I was baffled at first but I later discovered what he meant by that. It was not that I'd chosen partners who were bad people. I'd chosen partners who were not right for me and my reason for choosing them was not right either. Dr. Gordon also told me that I should possibly seek some counseling before I got involved with anyone else. He said that I needed healing. I agreed wholeheartedly. There had been so much trauma in my life in such a short time span. Some of it I brought upon myself and some, I did not. Nonetheless, I needed healing. I needed to know what was on the inside of me that caused me to make the choices I'd been making.

That was so hard for me to do because it, first of all, left me feeling like there was something seriously wrong with me. It also would cause me to take a long hard look in the mirror at myself and do some deep diving on the inside. It meant sharing my truth, the real me, with someone else, a stranger. Ultimately, it meant getting some answers that I probably would prefer not to hear. The truth hurts, maybe that's why so many of us opt to live a lie. Truth is, though, the truth heals, it delivers you and it sets you free. John 8:32 tells us, "You shall know the truth and the truth shall make you free."

As much as I wanted freedom, I didn't take the good Dr. Gordon's advice. I continued living and believing the lie. After all, there was nothing wrong with me. I just needed to choose better. I could control this thing. I now needed a list, not a type. This was what I began to tell myself. The list was very similar to the type just a little longer and perhaps I'd put a bit more thought and effort into it. Of course, the outcomes were more or less, the same. It didn't matter what was on the list. The problem was why I felt I wanted the things that were on the list. *What did those things mean to me? Did I really want these things or was it just popular, or did they only seem like a great idea at the time? Whose ideas are these anyway?* I questioned.

Often what we think we want, need, and desire in the perfect partner isn't really our ideas. Many times they come from what we see growing up at home with our parents or we see with couples on television and we want what we think our friends' relationships have and believe that's what we need. Sometimes even society will dictate the kind of partner we should choose for ourselves. That actually happens a lot more than we'd be willing to admit. There really isn't anything wrong with having a type, making a list, or having ideas about what it is that you want in your life partner. I would recommend, however, that you spend a lot of time getting to know yourself first. Get to know who you are. I mean who you really are. Discover things about yourself like: What do I like/dislike? What can I bring to the table or what do I have to offer someone? Am I a believer? Am I secure with myself? What are my strengths and weaknesses? Make a list about yourself. Do some deep diving and soul searching on yourself first. Take a long hard look in the mirror and then get down on your knees and ask God to reveal you to yourself, the real you. Ask Him to help you to accept the truth of whom you are and ask Him to help you become who He called you to be for the partner He has chosen for you. Truth is, if you don't know the truth about who you are, you can't know what you truly desire in anyone else.

First, partner with God. What kind of mask are you wearing? Stop looking like that. You know that, "who me?" look. Yes, you! We all wear a mask at times. Either you have worn a mask and you no longer are wearing it because you have had some divine revelation, intervention, or something like that, or, you are currently wearing a mask and you need a divine revelation or intervention, or, you will put on a mask at some point in your life, believe me.

PEEK-A-BOO: WHAT'S INSIDE OF YOU?

Here's the thing. You can't be afraid of what's behind the mask. Address it. Take off the mask and discover what it is. It may be a lot of different things like low self-esteem, victimization, rejection, or humiliation. It may be just one thing, but, until you know what it is, you won't be able to face it, own it, and allow God to heal you of it.

Have you ever had a friend or someone you could go to and tell them any and everything? They were always there to listen to you, your problems, and issues. You could trust them with anything you told them and they would be honest with you and always speak the truth about you and your situation. In my circle, that friend is me. I am by no means boasting but I am the one that folks could come to and they could tell me everything and I would help them navigate through. I could see so much in them and their situation but I couldn't see my own. I could literally help mend broken hearts and homes but I could not mend my own. I could spot jealousy, bitterness, resentment, and hatred a mile away, except I couldn't see it in me. I could walk you through overcoming your fears, help you to see the best in all things but I couldn't do any of that for myself. Why? I was wearing a mask. I didn't see it. I didn't want to see it. I was raised to be perfect. If I'm perfect then I clearly have no issues, right? No, that's absolutely wrong. I had issues and lots of them.

The funny thing is that some of us don't believe we have any issues at all, right? If we were being honest with ourselves, I'd say that we all have at least one issue. I finally realized that I kept ending up in the same place with every relationship. I mean, I'd have a new relationship with a new person in a new year but the outcome would ultimately be the same. I'm quite serious right now. It dawned on me that all things were new except for one thing. The only thing that had not changed ever was me.

So I was off to see the psychologist. Before I did that, I got down on my knees and I prayed. "Father God, it is me O Lord, standing in the need of prayer. I need you to help me, see me and then help me to discover what's inside me that causes me to do the things that I do and say and think. I need to know me because I keep ending up in the same place and I know that this is not what You desire for me so please help me." Now, this was my prayer. You certainly don't have to pray my prayer but prayer is a good place to start because it moves the hand of God. With that said friends, when you pray a prayer like that and you pray it with expectancy, then you need to make sure that you are ready for God to move, to give you what you were praying for.

God showed me, me. The mask came off. I wasn't ready, not at first. There's a saying, "You are what you eat." That's a little out there but, the truth is, there is some truth in that. The truth is that some things that happened to me early on in my life, didn't just happen to me; they became me, fear being the biggest culprit of all. I feared everything. I especially feared being abandoned because my daddy had left my mama and me when I was a young girl. There was insecurity because I didn't believe I was good enough, I felt inadequate.

The worst of them all may have been coming to terms with the fact that I was envious. That is not a good character trait to have, but, for me, it came from my dad choosing his new wife and her children over me. I was hurt and heartbroken. I was very jealous. These are just a few things that my unmasking revealed.

Trust me it will be hard to do, but it will change, possibly even save your life. I needed the healing for sure and I definitely did not want to continue ending up in the failed relationship junkyard, so I got vigilant about healing. Of course, God is the ultimate healer but know this, sometimes God will send you to the doctor for healing as well. Take note: He may even have the doctor prescribe you some medicine.

He sent me to a therapist and it was one of the best things that I could have ever done for myself. My therapist not only helped me to face certain things within me, but she helped me to understand how they came to be in the first place. Knowing is one thing, understanding is the beginning of healing and just in case you were wondering if it was successful, well, I guess you'll have to ask my husband of nearly 20 years.

Let's quickly touch on this because this is an actual thing and it's important too. Some things are in us possibly because it's something that has been passed down from generations. Oh yes! You may have heard of it before. It's commonly referred to as a generational curse. It is said that the effects of sin are naturally passed down from one generation to the next. When a father or mother has or had a sinful lifestyle, his or her children are likely to practice the same sinful lifestyle. This is actually implied in Exodus 20:5 which reads,

"You shall not bow down to them or serve them, for I The Lord your God am a jealous God, visiting the iniquity of the fathers on the children to the third and the fourth generations of those who hate me."

It's basically saying that the children will choose to repeat the sins of their parents. Oftentimes, the parents are teaching their children to do these things and don't even realize it themselves. In any case, you want to be mindful of this and go to God and ask Him to break the spirit of generational curses on your life, but when you do this, you need to do it with a repentant heart. 1 Samuel 12:10-11 reads,

"And they cried out to The Lord and said, We have sinned, because we have forsaken The Lord and have served the Baal's and the Ashtaroth. But now deliver us out of the hand of our enemies, that we may serve you. And The Lord sent Jerubbaal and Barak and Jephthah and Samuel and delivered you out of the hand of your enemies on every side and you lived in safety."

That's what we want. We want The Lord to deliver us from this curse that we may live, our children, children's children, and their children will live in safety.

The crazy thing is that sometimes, in fact, most of the time, we won't realize it right away. If I can be completely transparent with you and please don't judge me or my mama but I've had my four children who all had different fathers before I realized that my own mother had three children and that we all had different fathers as well. I laid down prostrate before The Lord and pleaded for Him. I prayed a prayer of repentance and asked for His forgiveness and I asked Him to break the curse of promiscuity, lust, adultery, and divorce that had been passed down from generation to generation in my family. I asked that it would be broken and not touch my children. I promised that if He closed that door, I'd never allowed it to be opened again. I wanted that and needed that to happen for me and my children.

Here's a little tip. When you pray, you need to be very specific about your needs and when you repent, be specific about what you are repenting for. He wants to hear it and you need to hear it to make sure that you don't turn back to it. And, just to circle back, when you are looking to choose a life partner or maybe you are just deciding who you'd like to date, get to know the real you, date yourself so to speak. Ask God to reveal what's behind door number "you." Unmask yourself. You deserve to be the best version of yourself and your intended partner deserves the best version of you as well.

Compatibility is also key. You can be the two most wonderful individuals in the world but not be the right wonderful people for each other. Oh yes! Compatibility is a real thing and it's really important too. So can you guess where I'm headed with this? The Bible says in 2 Corinthians 6:14, "Be ye not unequally yoked together with unbelievers; for what fellowship hath righteousness with unrighteousness? And what communion hath light with darkness?" Basically, the two have nothing in common; they are not a compatible pair. So again, just because you are the best of the best, you just might not be the best for each other. That's why knowing who you truly are is so crucial, inside and

PEEK-A-BOO: WHAT'S INSIDE OF YOU?

out. Get to know you, boo!

Chapter Reflection:

"Some say that if we do not learn from our mistakes we are bound to repeat them. Likewise if we do not understand why we do the things we do, we are likely to do them over and over again."

Read and Meditate:

    2 Corinthians 13:5

    Ephesians 3:17

    James 1:24

    Romans 7:19

Chapter 4

Not Good Enough?

"Sometimes life throws us one or more curve balls that majorly disrupts our lives. What matters most is to use these issues of life as stepping stones to obtain freedom and always live in a state of repentance, forgiveness of others and of self. This will allow peace to flow like a river in your soul to gain strength, courage and power to run the race with confidence, grace and dignity."
Felicia Permillion

Be mighty careful of that phrase, "I'd never do that," because you might do that and a whole lot more than that too. Growing up in a Christian home and also going to an all girls' Catholic school, you tend to hear things that other folks get into, that you swear that you'd never do yourself. It's not cool I know, but if we are all being honest and, I do pride myself on being an honest person, we all can be a little bit judgy at times. Sometimes after church, we'd get home, and no sooner than we walked through the door one of the church sisters was calling to tell the latest gossip to my mama. I'd hear them talking about who had told a lie, who was stealing, who was cheating, who was having sex out of wedlock, you name it. Stuff was going on and they'd talk about it and I'd say to myself, *I'd never do that*. The same thing would happen at school. I'd hear about the drama between friends and their boyfriends. There would be hook-ups, drinking, smoking, and not just cigarettes, pregnancies, threesomes, and all kinds of nonsense that I swore on ten stacks of Bibles I'd never do.

Remember, I mentioned that I was Daddy's perfect girl? I really was a good, good girl when I was younger. Not that I'm a bad person now, but there was a time when things got a little sticky when my actions were somewhat questionable, so I minded my p's and q's and did what he told me to do and that was it. About the time that Daddy left home, however, there was a bit of a shift in my character. I suppose I may not have told him or anyone else for that matter, how I really felt about Daddy leaving but it definitely showed in my actions. Now I wasn't just blatantly wilding out, we couldn't do that back then. Parents in those days would have put a hurting on you. It was still legal to whoop your kids and the punishments were worse than the actual whooping. They seemed more like life sentences. Today kids get things taken away like their cell phones and video games for about a week. Back then we'd get everything except our breath taken away for an entire year. I remember my daddy unplugged my phone in my bedroom once for running the bill up to $500 talking to my friend up north and he didn't give it back for months. Kids would be punished from playing outside and, by the time you saw them again, you thought they were brand new neighbors; they would have been in the house for so long. Things are very different now. In those days we did our dirt in secret. We hid our transgressions or at least we'd better try to hide them if we knew what was good for us.

Are you familiar with the phrase, "One thing leads to another?" There is definitely a lot of truth in that. I mean I remember when I and my sister-friends would sneak out and go to the park where the boys hung out. That led to going over to the boys' houses. We didn't do anything forbidden, but we also knew our parents wouldn't necessarily like us being at the boys' house. We would just put on our skates and we'd show up on their street and oftentimes at their front door. We knew better and, if Daddy found out that we'd gone to a boy's house, we'd all be in big trouble for sure. That's what the fast girls did, not us or so that's what they thought.

From there we started sneaking our friends into the house, including the boys when our parents weren't home, but, as soon as we'd hear a car pull up and the door shut, we'd sneak everyone out of the window on the side of the house where the dogs were. That was actually quite funny to see them trying their darndest to get over that wall before they were bitten.

Now, this may seem pretty innocent or not but, one thing would lead to the next and things were escalating. I'd never dreamed that I would actually sneak a boy into my house, doing what I said I'd never do and, most importantly, doing something that my parents would have never agreed to.

As the years went by and my personal pain grew deeper and the hole in my heart grew bigger, the less perfect I became or even wanted to be. So it continued and one imperfect deed continued to lead to another imperfect deed. Smoking a little pot with my sister led to drinking a little beer with my friends in the park. Having sex at 16 years of age eventually led to getting pregnant at 16 years of age. Becoming pregnant led to an abortion, something that I definitely said that I would never do and when I did it, I vowed to never do it again and…Do you see where I'm going with this?

None of us when we are just little children say things like, "I wanna get high on pot and booze when I grow up." We don't have dreams about having premarital sex and aborting our babies before we are really ready to become moms. These, more than likely, are the result of one teeny tiny offense leading to the next bigger offense and oftentimes these offenses are birthed out of our own pain, usually pain that we didn't cause ourselves. That was certainly the case for me anyway.

Have you ever had, "buyer's remorse?" I would always ask God to forgive me because I had remorse and I did feel convicted by The Holy Spirit for the things that I'd done that I knew went against God. I didn't really want to do all of those things or become the person I was becoming, but, the pain at times was unbearable and it was growing worse. I continued to do the things I was doing, sometimes hurting others, but mostly hurting myself. At one point I felt that I'd done way too much. I thought that my sins at this point were just downright unforgivable. They were way too many. I mean why would God forgive me? I couldn't even forgive myself. I was ashamed of myself. I started to really dislike me, and because I didn't like me, it was hard to believe that anyone else could or should, even God. I thought very little of myself.

The once perfect Daddy's girl was now quite far from being perfect in any way, shape, form, or fashion. My light used to shine so brightly and now it was quite dim. It was a very sad time for me. Pain doesn't only promote bad behavior but it also contributes to bad and lethal thinking. Guilt from all of the craziness that was going on led to the feeling of being unworthy of anything good in my life, especially love. Anything bad or negative that would happen to me, I started to feel like I deserved it. If I were in a relationship with someone and things went awry, I would automatically think that it was my fault that it didn't work out. If I struggled with finances, if I didn't get the job, if I didn't get chosen for the promotion or the deal didn't go through, I thought it was because I didn't deserve it. I was unworthy. I was simply not good enough.

It felt like there was a dark cloud hanging over my head. Have you ever lived in that place? You honestly start to believe that you are damaged goods and that God is done with you. Scary as…you know what. Again, it's like you have fallen into this black hole. It's dark, deep, cold, and you are alone and you can't get out. This time you are really trying to get out, though. You are not necessarily screaming out for help. You are so paralyzed by the pain that you just stay stuck. In fact, instead of trying to get out of the situation, you don't look up; you don't cry out for help, you start to just succumb to the pain and dig yourself deeper in the hole. Of course, now you feel all alone and you begin to fade into the background.

Now I want you to listen very closely to what I'm about to tell you because it's real, real important. This right here will help you. I wish someone would have told me this a lot sooner, but God's timing is always best. There is a reason why God allows us to go through the things we go through. Remember that there is always a purpose and He always has the perfect plan for your life. All you have to do is trust and believe Him, period.

Did you know that God loves you so much that there is absolutely nothing you can do to make Him so angry with you that He'd stop loving you? Romans 8:35 says this,

"Can anything ever separate us from Christ's love? Does it mean He no longer loves us if we have trouble or calamity, or are persecuted, or hungry or destitute, or in danger, or threatened with death?"

Wait a minute, because that's not all of it. It goes on to say this in verses 38 and 39,

"And I am convinced that nothing can ever separate us from God's love. Neither death nor life, neither angels nor demons, neither our fears for today nor our worries about tomorrow, not even the powers of hell can separate us from God's love. No power in the sky above or in the earth below, indeed, nothing in all creation will be able to separate us from the love of God that is revealed in Christ Jesus, our Lord."

So if that's a bit too complex for you to understand, allow me to break it down like this. The definition of the word "nothing" is this according to Merriam Webster; "No single thing, not anything." That means that all of the lying, stealing, cheating, smoking, boozing, your bitterness, resentment and enviousness, the premarital out-of-wedlock sexcapades, the abortion, gossiping, plotting, and scheming, cannot and will not stop Him from loving you. Nothing! Not a single thing, not anything! He created us because He loves us and there is absolutely nothing that we can do about it, not a single thing, not anything.

But wait, there's more."What about forgiveness? Doesn't that mean that He will forgive me for my sins and past mistakes?" Oh, but it most certainly does, my friends. In Matthew, Jesus says that we should forgive each other seventy times seven times. That number symbolizes boundlessness and by the way, that's forgiving each person seventy times seven daily. You do the math. Now, if He is requiring forgiveness from us to one another, do you honestly think that He would not also hold himself to such a standard when it comes to Him forgiving us? Of course, He would. He's just that kind of God. 1 John 1:9 clearly states, "If we confess our sins, He is faithful and just to forgive us our sins and to cleanse us from all unrighteousness." Psalms 103:10-14 blesses us in that it reads,

"He hath not dealt with us after our sins; nor rewarded us according to our iniquities. For as the heaven is high above the earth so great is His mercy toward them that fear him. As far as the east is from the west, so far hath He removed our transgressions from us."

Not only does our Sovereign God forgive us for our mess-ups and forgets them forever. In Hebrew 8:12, He says that He will also be merciful toward them.

Friends, when you find yourself feeling hopeless and in despair, I encourage you to meditate on these things daily. This is the infallible Word of The Lord. It is true and gives life. It is the light in that dark hole that you have fallen into. Follow the light and trust that it will lead you to freedom.

God, you are good. Even before Jesus stepped down from heaven and came to earth. He knew what His assignment was going to entail. He knew that He was coming to save us from our sins and redeem us back unto the Father. Here's the kicker, He died for all sin. He died for the sins that had been committed, that were being committed, and all the sins that would ever be committed. All sins were nailed to the cross over 2,000-years-ago, all of it when Jesus was crucified. Our debt was paid in full. That doesn't mean that it's okay to just do whatever because we've already been forgiven. **No**!!! That's not at all what I am saying.

Here's the thing, sin is a result of a bad choice or choices. God gave us all free will. This means that we are given free will to make our own decisions. We can choose from the Tree of Life or we can choose from the Tree of the Knowledge of Good and Evil. In other words, we can choose good or bad, life or death. The choice is always ours but so are the consequences.

Just because He forgives us for our sins and actually forgets them forever when we confess our sins, there are still consequences for our choices. I don't want you to miss this. If there is a struggle in your life because of a choice you made, it's not because God doesn't love you, it's a consequence. If you feel as if you are praying and He's not listening because He hasn't answered you, well, first of all, God always answers prayers. That doesn't mean He's written you off or that He's not listening to you. He may not give you an answer in the nanosecond that you were expecting but He always answers prayers. Truth is our God wants only for us to be happy, to live this life that He has blessed us with to the absolute fullest. He wants the purpose that He has placed down on the inside of you to be fulfilled on the earth. One of my favorite scriptures teaches us this in John 3:16, "For God so loved the world, that He gave His only Son, that whoever believes in Him should not perish but have eternal life."

Because of Jesus, His death, burial, and His resurrection, when the Father looks at us He sees His righteous, holy, and beloved Son. Because of Jesus, we are forgiven, because of Jesus we are whole, because of Jesus we have been set free. We have been washed in the blood of the lamb, we are redeemed, and we are good enough because we are His.

For me, this is something that I still struggle with because, in a world that constantly reminds you of your past mistakes and failures, in a world that delights itself in comparisons, in a world where anything goes and everything and everyone is accepted except for you, it's hard sometimes to remember who you are and that you are good enough. You can so easily get caught up in trying to please people, which is utterly impossible, by the way, and then you fall back into that mindset if the people don't think I'm good enough then, of course, God doesn't think so either.

That kind of thinking is completely backward, of course. We should not be living for the approval and applause of people but rather for the audience of one and that one is our Lord and Savior, Jesus Christ. See it's my flesh that causes me to digress. I've learned to wake up every day and die to my flesh so that I can truly live in Jesus Christ. I read the Word of God and that helps bring me back to the place of knowing who I am and although I may not be perfect and yes, I may choose from the wrong tree sometimes, still I am good enough. As long as there is breath in my body, blood flowing through my veins, my heart still beats, and all of my organs are functioning the way He designed them to, even if I fall, there is still purpose. If I am blessed to see another sunrise if my name is on the roll call another day and if I should happen to miss the mark, there's still promise. God's mercies are new every day. Lamentations 3:22-23 says it best, "The steadfast love of The Lord never ceases; His mercies never come to an end; they are new every morning, great is your faithfulness." The more you get to really know who God is, the more you'll discover how much He truly loves you and knows just who you are in the Kingdom of God. Know this today my friend, you are good enough for Him and that's all that matters.

Chapter Reflection

"God gave us an entire book that tells us how much He loves us and that we are more than enough but it only takes one Instagram post to convince us otherwise."

Read and Meditate:

Genesis 1:27

Isaiah 49:16

Romans 8:16-17

1 Peter 2:9

1 John 3:1

Chapter 5

When Faced With Infertility

"Keep your heart open for what God has planned for you. 'Not now' doesn't mean never. Over the years I've learned to let go of what I thought my life was supposed to be and celebrate all of the goodness my life is now."
Danine Henry

WHEN FACED WITH INFERTILITY

My granddaughter says that when she grows up she wants to be a mommy just like her mommy. Many of us have been asked what it is we want to be when we grow up and quite possibly some of us want the same as my little Nell. All that you've ever dreamt about is being a mommy, to have your baby to love. Perhaps, it was not really a dream for you. Perhaps, you kind of always thought that it comes along with being a woman and that, once you grow up and get married, the natural order of things is to then have a baby. We think it's just what we women were born to do. If I'm honest, I think that I probably assumed as much myself. I mentioned earlier that I actually didn't want any children initially but I'm pretty sure I believed that, having them was as simple as having unprotected sex without taking any birth control. It's what women were created to do, or so I thought. As you read earlier, I had some complications with having children. Some would call it a form of infertility. I had two stillborn births. My problem was never getting pregnant. I did that easily. My problem was not carrying my babies to term. I was delivering stillborn. My babies were not born alive. Technically speaking, I wasn't infertile. I was quite fertile, in fact.

There are many women, however, who cannot and are not getting pregnant. For many of them, this fate is worse than disease and death. Coming home from the hospital twice without a baby, for me, left me feeling like a total failure, as if I were broken or something. Some women have similar feelings when they are not able to conceive. She thinks, "What's wrong with me?" She believes that she has failed as a woman and a spouse. She often begins to feel very insecure. Perhaps, most of her friends have children or her parents are putting pressure on her to have children because they want to be grandparents. Or maybe even a promise was made to her spouse to have children but more than likely she has just waited her entire life to finally be a mommy and seemingly, that was not going to happen.

 I had absolutely no idea what a test tube baby or IVF, aka, In Vitro Fertilization, was. I'd heard people use these terms but I was clueless as to what it actually meant. I literally did not know the subject. When my oldest was just about to graduate high school and go to the military, it scared me because the time had gone by so fast and I realized that I'd worked so hard and so much, I'd missed my baby growing into a young man and now he was leaving the nest. I was devastated but I knew one thing. I had two other children at home at that time and I was not going to miss out on them growing up. I did what I felt I had to do, and so I changed careers. I went from having a career in the fashion industry for more than 20 years to a career in healthcare, infertility to be exact.

WHEN FACED WITH INFERTILITY

If anyone would have told me that I would have left the fashion industry, I would have rebuked that spirit in the name of Jesus Christ. I had always loved fashion and I never dreamed of doing anything else, but God has His own plans for our lives indeed. Be sure to write that down if you are taking notes. I think, no, I know, that this new chapter of my life is where I started walking into my purpose, the purpose that God had placed on the inside of me. Little did I know that I would begin to speak life into the lives of other women and encourage and empower them. I soon realized that my own experience with infertility wasn't about me as much as it was about God setting me up to use me as a vessel to do His good work, which was to encourage other women who would walk through this valley. God is so amazing like that. Most of what we go through are never about us. What we go through, the hurt, the pain, the disappointments, and everything in between, is all about advancing the Kingdom of God. Take the Bible for instance and all of its wonderful stories. Someone would go through something and we can glean from their experiences, right? They endured and even today, are helping all of us to overcome.

On my very first day in my new career, I thought that there was no way I'd ever be able to learn all of this. It was as if I was reading and hearing a foreign language. My hair felt as if it were on fire because my brain had exploded. But just like that, because this was not about me but Him, this is where God wanted me to be. I was on assignment for Him. I began speaking that language fluently and started teaching others, even doctors. It was all a part of God's plan.

While working at the infertility practice it seemed that my faith began to grow deeper and deeper. I was already walking with The Lord but I had this thirst, this hunger as I'd never had before. After working with the practice for a few years, God led me to go to The School of Ministry. I was literally being led by the Holy Spirit. He was taking me deeper. I had no idea at the time why I was enrolling but I did it anyway. I even thought at one point that I shouldn't do it because I was just going to fail. Not only did I not fail but I graduated among the top of my class. It was about that time that there would be a shift in my assignment. I went from not knowing if I could actually learn about infertility myself, to being able to educate doctors on the subject of infertility and about how our group of experts could help their patients achieve a family, to speaking to and educating the patients directly. This was a whole other layer. This was when God opened up the opportunity for me to speak life and to encourage His daughters and sometimes His sons as well.

I was often asked by women, "Do you think I'll ever be able to have a baby of my own?" Bringing to mind my own experience, I'd often say in response,

"You know that I am unable to promise anything, however, I do know that all things are possible. It may not happen the way you always dreamed, expected, or wanted it to happen, but, if it's meant to happen, it can." I'd encourage them to have faith and to live in a positive space. I'd tell them that if they are given to prayer, then by all means pray. Those words, even to the non-believer, seemed to be of great comfort. I would sometimes be asked if I had ever gone through anything like this before. I knew that was just God opening a window of opportunity for me to share my experiences about the loss of my children and the good news of how He blessed me and gave me double for my trouble. I'd lost two babies, a boy first and then a girl, and He in turn gave me four beautiful healthy children. Sometimes all people need is a little hope, the kind of hope that heals.

Just so that we are all clear, according to WHO; World Health Organization, the definition of infertility is, "A disease of the reproductive system defined by the failure to achieve a clinical pregnancy after 12 months or more of unprotected sexual intercourse."[1] For many, it means not being able to produce or give birth to a live baby. So not

---

[1] World Health Organization, Infertility Definitions and Terminology, www.who.int (accessed January 9, 2020)

that a woman isn't able to conceive or get pregnant, as with me, isn't her problem, it's actually losing the baby during the course of the pregnancy before there is an actual live birth, that is causing her situation to be looked upon as being infertile or having infertility.

Miscarriage is a very difficult thing for a woman. Here are a few facts on the matter: According to the March of Dimes,

"As many as 50% of all pregnancies end in miscarriage, most often before a woman misses a menstrual period or even knows she is pregnant. About 15-25% of recognized pregnancies will end in a miscarriage. More than 80% of miscarriages occur within the first three months of pregnancy."[2]

This is really something to consider when feeling that, because I am a woman, I am also supposed to be a mother or be able to have a baby, easily. The fact is, the Bible tells us in Genesis, that God created women to be helpmates. That does not translate into mothers. The scripture says in Genesis 2:18, "Then the Lord God said, 'It is not good that the man should be alone.' I will make him a helper fit for Him." Also, if we continue to read on in the Bible, we will come across many actually

---

[2] March of Dimes, Miscarriage Key Points, November 2017, www.marchofdimes.org (accessed January 9, 2021)

barren women. They too suffered from infertility in some form. With that said, many of them eventually were able to conceive and deliver live babies. There was even a woman later in Genesis by the name of Sarai. She was sterile for many, many years. Actually, the Bible tells us that she was 90-years-old when The Lord finally opened her womb so that she would conceive. God had told her husband that she would be, "A mother of many nations," and that she would conceive and bear a son but Sarai did not believe this. She actually laughed at the notion. How could this happen since nearly three decades had passed since God told Abraham that they would have a son? He kept His promise to them and it came to pass just as He'd said. If He says it, He will surely do it. Genesis 21:1-4 says it like this, "The Lord came back to visit Sarai as He said He would, and He kept His promise to her. At exactly the time God said it would happen, Sarai became pregnant and gave birth to a son for Abraham in his old age. Sarai was 90-years-old and her husband Abraham was 100-years-old. Now I'm not suggesting that you will be 90-years-old before God blesses you with a baby. That was way back then, but what I am suggesting or would like to impress upon you is that no matter what it looks like or how long it's been, no matter the odds stacked up against you, no matter what it is, if God says that He's going to do it, you can consider it done.

Now back to the question of women being

created to be mothers. We were created, most of us to be able to conceive and have children. What I mean is, we were born with the essential reproductive anatomy to have children but that, in and of itself, does not mean that we all were created to be someone's mother, to have a child of our own. That's a promise that was never made to women. Here's the thing though, if it is your heart's desire, then go to Him in prayer and make your request known to Him. Read Philippians 4:6. It says this, "Be anxious for nothing, but in everything, by prayer and petition, with thanksgiving, present your requests to God." Another one to follow that up with is in Psalms 37:4 and it says thank you, Jesus, "Take delight in the Lord, and He will give you the desires of your heart." And just one more for you that I know will bless your spirit. It's found in Joshua 23:14, "Now behold, today I am going the way of all the earth and you know in all your hearts and all your souls that not one word of all the good words which the Lord our God spoke concerning you has failed; all have been fulfilled for you, not one of them has failed." Change the word, "word" to "promise" and read it again. Did it bless you? I knew it would.

I've spoken to many women and men and have had more than a few friends that experienced infertility in various forms. Some have not yet been able to achieve a family. Some of them are praying and waiting on God patiently. Some have given up on the idea altogether. Others used their resources and found other ways to achieve their family; In Vitro Fertilization, egg donors, surrogates, adoption and/or fostering children. If you have prayed, or maybe God told you in a dream that you would be a mommy, don't throw in the towel or be dismayed when it doesn't come to pass the way you thought it would. Don't put limits on God or place him in your box. God is almighty, He's sovereign and can do the absolutely impossible because He's God. If you've trusted Him for one thing in your life, know that you can trust Him for all things in your life. If I may, let me share with you a couple of stories.

I have this friend and all her life she dreamt of being a mommy. When she grew up, she got married and did what seemed logical. She began to plan for her family. They tried their hardest to have a baby but they miscarried many times. Unfortunately, the marriage succumbed to the sadness and disappointment of not being able to conceive, which ultimately led to many other problems and ended in divorce. My friend, as a single woman, still wanted her heart's desire, which was to be a mommy. We'd have many conversations about options. She started going to church and she prayed and the years just went by quickly. She became depressed, stressed, and thought about just giving up. She said that not only has this been her dream but one Sunday at church God made her a promise that she'd have a baby. I told her that if that's true, God doesn't break promises and it may not happen the way she'd imagined, but she would become a mother. Today she is the mother of twins, two beautiful children.

Another friend came to the fertility practice that I worked for. We had many discussions about her situation and the services, reputation, and successes of my practice. She was very well-versed with In Vitro Fertilization. Although she knew that would more than likely be the answer, she wasn't really prepared for her specific options. She wanted a child of her own, meaning using her eggs. When she was given the expert opinion of one of our founding physicians, she simply said no and sought other advice which I would have too probably. She was told the same thing by other expert physicians in the field. This was not God saying **no**. **This was God saying not thy will but my will be done. Remember, He has a purpose and a perfect plan for our lives. He makes no mistakes. He knows all about it and He cares for every one of us.** Needless to say, my dear friend trusted God and His process. She is the mother of a handsome and healthy son. Infertility sometimes happens, but it does not have the final say as to whether or not you will have a baby or be a mother. God has the final say. God is bigger than infertility too.

Chapter Reflection

"Many things happen in life that we don't understand. God knows and He cares deeply for you. Motherhood can happen in many ways. Delayed does not mean denied."

Read and Meditate:

Psalms 34:17-20

Philippians 4:19

Isaiah 40:1

Zechariah 9:12

Job 42:10

Chapter 6

Panic and Anxiety with a Side of Depression

"You can't have faith and worry at the same, choose faith."
Nina Jones

I remember that day very well. I was cruising down the main strip with my then-husband on a beautiful Sunday afternoon, listening to the music on the car stereo and we were taking in all the interesting sights. I remember it because the day before that was Saturday and I'd spent the entire day in the beauty shop getting my hair and nails done. I was feeling good and looked good too, at least I thought so. There was no drama going on between us and things were really cool. Then all of a sudden, without any warning at all, this bigger than life wave of fear overcame my body. The feeling was a feeling of sheer dread. My hands had become clammy and my breath was really short. My heart started beating faster and faster. I could honestly hear it beating. I looked down at my chest and I could actually see my blouse vibrating from my heartbeat. I thought I was going to die at that very moment. I was so afraid that I couldn't even speak. The fear had paralyzed me. I just wanted him to quickly get me home. I didn't tell him exactly what was going on because he'd freak out and that wouldn't have been good for anyone. I just asked him to take me home because I wasn't feeling so well and so he did.

Once I arrived at home, I immediately jumped in a hot bath because no matter what's going on, no matter how bad it is, a hot bath makes everything all right. Soon after, I began to feel like my normal self again but that was one of the scariest things that had ever happened to me. It felt like I was having a heart attack. I told no one.

    Being in school at this time, school required me to work 20 hours per week in my field which was fashion marketing and merchandising. I got a part-time job in retail working as a visual merchandiser at a children's store. Each day after my classes, I'd go to work. Merchandising came pretty easily for me; I could do it in my sleep. I've always been extremely neat, detail-oriented, and organized. Part of my job was to unpack the shipment and stock and restock merchandise on the sales floor. I would also change out all the mannequins and build and rebuild sections in the various departments so that it always popped and stayed relevant. I absolutely loved it and I was quite good at it too. One afternoon, in particular, things would not go so smoothly for me. It started as a pretty normal day at the store. I'd just started my shift and I'd begun to pull merchandise from the stockroom to restock the sales floor. I found myself knee-deep in any and everything that one could buy for their newborn baby. Of course, after just having lost my baby, this could have been tough for me but I truly believed that I was fine. I honestly thought that I had accepted what happened and that I had already moved on and put losing the baby behind me. There I stood, standing in the middle of the department folding baby T-shirts, gowns, and blankets when I began to feel clammy and a little faint, which immediately scared the daylights out of me. These symptoms sound minor I know but I just felt a bit off. My heart started to do that thing again. It started beating faster and faster. Once again, I was short of breath and this time, the room began to spin. I couldn't breathe. I needed to get out of there fast.

I went to my manager and made up an excuse that I got my period and that I needed to rush home. I didn't even wait for permission, I just ran out of the store. Once I was outside and I could feel the wind on my face, I started to calm down and feel like myself again. I was able to regulate my breathing on my own, in and out slowly. My heart slowed down to its normal pace and I was even able to drive myself home safely. Just when I thought that the first incident was a one-time deal, it had happened again. Of course, it did. That's just how my life was. This fear was gripping, terrifying. It felt as if I were actually going to die. Still, I told no one.

The incidents, as I so lovingly referred to them, had started to become more and more frequent. They'd happen when I was alone or in public with friends. I could be at school, at church, or even driving in my car all alone, and out of nowhere, fear would hit me like a ton of bricks. I tried asking God to just take it away but He did not. Finally, I decided that I needed to go to the doctor. I had started to think that I had a heart condition. I was born with a severe heart murmur. Perhaps it had returned. I made an appointment to see our family physician. If I have not mentioned it before, I have extreme white coat syndrome. I was terribly afraid of doctors. I was always afraid of doctors as a little girl. This thing was serious though and I had to get to the bottom of it.

At the doctor's office, Dr. Miller hooked me up to an EKG machine. After a few minutes, my results were ready. "Well, you don't seem to be having a heart attack but your heart is beating quite rapidly," Dr. Miller responded. He asked what was bothering me or what was it that was causing me to be so nervous and afraid. I had no idea. In my mind, I was completely fine but obviously, my body did not agree at all. Now, to this day I don't take any western medication of any kind unless the situation is dire. There is the occasional Tylenol for monthly cramps but, that day, Dr. Miller had prescribed something to help me sleep, something to calm me down. He also made an appointment for me to see a specialist, a cardiologist. I was certainly afraid of that but I had to do it. When I saw the cardiologist and after he'd also given me an EKG test, he told me that my heart was strong and seemingly in good condition but it was, in fact, beating rather fast, so he decided to monitor my heart for 24 hours and then sent me home with a heart monitor. At this point, there was no way for me to hide the fact that I was wearing a heart monitor from anyone, so I finally informed my mother as to what had been going on. I explained the incidents of heart palpitations I'd been experiencing, the shortness of breath, spinning rooms, feeling faint, and the clammy hands. Mama looked at me and her eyes filled with tears. She cried and said that she was so sorry that she had given this to me. I didn't understand what she meant and then she told me that she had been struggling with panic attack disorder (PAC) most of her life and she feared that she has passed it on to me. She said that it had affected her to the point of nearly ruining her life. She believed it had a lot to do with the problems she and my daddy had and it was partly to blame for her marriage ending. She told me that I had to gain control or "it" would take over and control every aspect of my life. *Oh no, I was not about to let that happen.* The next day I returned to the cardiologist who told me that everything looked good. He did however give me the name of another doctor that I could go see if I felt I needed another opinion or if the incidents continued.

Have you ever tried to just wish something away? Well, that certainly wasn't working for me. Mama was right though. I had to take control of these panic attacks. They were happening more frequently than before and were really starting to get on my nerves. They even started happening in my sleep. These panic attacks are called, "night terrors." I'd be in bed falling asleep and then all of a sudden I'd wake up feeling like something had just spooked me. It's hard to describe but it would seem as if I'd been asleep for some time but in reality, it would have only been for like five or ten minutes. This continued to happen for hours. Sometimes I'd be in a deep sleep and I'd wake up spooked and the room would be spinning, my heart would be racing and I couldn't catch my breath. I'd have this awful feeling of doom looming over me. It was awfully scary. I felt not only like I was going to die right then and there, I felt like I was losing my mind. I was definitely losing sleep and I was definitely not in control of this thing, rather it was starting to control every aspect of me. Mama had warned me. Nothing I did was working. I even asked God to please make it stop. I don't think He was listening to me. If I'm honest, most of what I was doing, though, was worrying. So, I began to fall back, became a recluse. I didn't want to be around friends or my family anymore. I was embarrassed and ashamed. I felt like a freak. I just stayed home and let fear settle its ugly self in and get real comfortable in my house.

Eventually, enough was enough, and believe me when I tell you; I'd had enough of this nonsense. I made an appointment with that doctor that the cardiologist had told me about. I needed a second opinion and most importantly, I needed it to stop! It could not have me anymore. I was done. I arrived at my appointment not knowing really what to expect. The sign on the door read, "Internal Medicine." I had no idea what exactly that meant and how it was going to help my condition but I would soon find out. For someone who was totally afraid of white coats, I'd definitely seen more than a few within a very short span but it had to be done.

The doctor was an older gentleman, maybe in his late 60's or 70's. He took his time carefully studying my records. He asked questions as he read. He never touched me at all. He didn't even listen to my heart. There were no machines or monitors, just him and I. He finally looked up from my file and said, "It seems to me you are having some pretty major anxiety attacks."

I said, "Yes sir, I am." For some reason, I just began to sob like a baby. I was so tired and said, "I just want my life back. Can you make this stop?"

I never shall forget his response. He looked at me with those soft-grey eyes and said, "I could easily prescribe some medication, Prozac or Xanax but the problem is that you would more than likely have to take that medication for the rest of your life and you are much too young, that would be a long, long time." He then said, "The other problem with that is that you won't ever know or understand why you are having these panic attacks and therefore never truly be healed from the real illness. Instead, I'm going to prescribe this for you." He scribbled something on the Rx tablet, ripped off the sheet, and handed it to me. The prescription was to, "pray," plain and simple. He said every chance I got and especially when the fear and anxiety would begin to rise inside me, just begin to pray. He told me to pray every day until it goes away. He was the best doctor and the best prescription ever. He will never know how valuable his words were to me and I did exactly what he said.

Things got a whole lot worse before they got better. I started becoming fearful of everything because it just wasn't going away fast enough. The fear and anxiety were still with me as my skin. I was praying just as the doctor had prescribed. I prayed every day and every night. I prayed in and out of season. I prayed without ceasing. I prayed in the car, in the shower, and the bed. In my mind, it felt as if maybe God was mad at me for some reason. He wasn't hearing me or simply not listening to me anymore. My prayers didn't deserve to be heard. The thought of God not listening to me anymore was the scariest feeling of all. Again, I felt all alone. The walls were starting to close in on me and thoughts of death were playing on a loop over and over in my mind. *Is today going to be the day, the day that I die? God didn't let my babies live, He wants me to die too.* In hindsight that sounded so ridiculous but at the time it was so real in my mind. I was absolutely convinced that God didn't love me and wanted me to die. Every day when I woke up I wondered if it were going to be my last. This was depressing. I was weak and felt completely hopeless. *Was this really my fate?*

Well, just like God puts rainbows in the sky, He put an angel in my life. My mama was that angel. One night I had an awful night of terror. I was at my home, Mama was at hers. I jumped out of the bed, grabbed the phone, and ran outside to get some air because I felt like I couldn't breathe at all. I called her and told her that I couldn't breathe and that my heart was racing, beating so fast. Mama's voice was just like that of an angel. She said, "Honey, just try and calm down." She spoke softly and slowly so that my level of anxiety would mimic hers. She told me to take a deep breath and let it out real slow. She totally helped to calm my breathing and pace my heart. I could feel the panic attack passing. Mama said, "Honey, although it feels like you are going to absolutely die, I need you to know that you absolutely are **not**." She gave me some helpful tips to battle panic, anxiety and fear, like making sure I had water next to my bed, keeping lavender under my pillow, and drinking lavender tea before going to bed.

The most valuable tip she gave me was this. She said that what the doctor had told me was correct. I needed to pray this thing away. Mama said that there was just one thing missing on that prescription tablet and that was, I needed to read the Word of God as well. Mama told me to pray God's Words over my life and then watch what God would do. I tell you what, when I put the doctor's prescription and Mama's tips together, especially reading the Word of God and praying it over my life, it changed my life forever. Do I still sometimes have panic and anxiety attacks? Sure do, but I know that I'm not going to die. I know that God hears me, He sees me, and He's right there with me always. Mama's gone home to be with God now, so it's not her voice that calms the storm in me, it's His. Instead of just a glass of water by my bedside, I have His Word too. I sip and read, sip, and read until He rocks me back to sleep.

I came to understand why I was having these awful panic attacks. I believed that my children died because God was angry at me and punishing me and therefore I was going to die too. Reading the Word of God helped me to realize that this simply was not the truth at all and it was not God. The Word taught me that my Heavenly Father loves me and that He Himself is the very essence of love and He sent His only begotten Son to die on a cross so that I would live. The words in Romans 5:8 helped me then and still do today, "God demonstrates His own love for us in this: While we were still sinners, Christ died for us." God didn't want me to die. He wanted me to live and to live life abundantly, not in fear. 2 Timothy 1:7 told me, "For God hath not given us the spirit of fear; but of power, love and a sound mind."

My fear did not come from God, not only that but He gave me a spirit of power to conquer the very fear that I had. He also gave me the spirit of a sound mind.

Though it felt as if I were losing my mind, I actually had the power to take my peace and sound mind back. Doesn't that just give you life? Those words gave me my life back. So yes, The Lord decided to take my babies home with Him and He had His reasons for that. It was all according to His perfect will and plan for my life and I trust Him. Praise be to God I am still here!!! This does not mean that I don't have panic attacks and anxiety from time to time. I just don't have them nearly as often as I once did. Now that I know where they come from or should I say, who they come from, I'm no longer afraid. Fear no longer has a grip on me. I may not always be in control of the ailments that attack my body and mind, but I am in full control of how I respond to them. My response is the Word of God. If you are struggling with fear, panic, anxiety, and depression, try God's Word.

Chapter Reflection

"Fear is the root of panic, anxiety, and depression. Fear is not of God so command it to flee in Jesus's name and be free."

Read and Meditate:

    Isaiah 43:1

    Psalms 34:4-5

    Psalms 23:4

    Psalms 27:1

    Philippians 4:6

Chapter 7

Battlefield of the Mind

- "When a mom learns her child is living with a mental health challenge, her peace can only be found through her relationship with The Holy Redeemer." - Gigi Crowder, L.E., Executive Director NAMI Contra Costa

"He's having a hard time staying in his seat," the vice-principal began telling us about our son, Cody who was a freshman in high school at the time. He said that our boy was extremely smart, there was no doubt there. He'd aced every test he had taken and the work that he did was exceptional. He just could not stay in his seat and he was set on being the class clown for sure. We were told that he taps the desk with his pencil constantly and that he was forever using the trash can as his own personal basketball hoop. For this reason, the vice-principal felt that perhaps he was too immature for high school and perhaps we should have him see the school psychologist regularly. My husband and I were very new to all this, so of course, we spoke with the school psychologist. We wanted our children to be as successful as they possibly could be in school. The school psychologist told us she had tested Cody, without our knowledge or consent, and that he scored very high for ADD and ADHD. Both of which are the exact same thing. Attention Deficit Disorder (ADD) is a developmental disorder characterized by symptoms of inattention such as distractibility, disorganization, or forgetfulness, or symptoms of hyperactivity and impulsivity such as fidgeting, speaking out of turn, or restlessness. *Huh*, I thought!

We'd noticed that Cody was in fact quite hyperactive, he was always moving. He was very athletic, so most of his movements were in sports but even off the field or court, yes, he was always doing something. He has some interesting habits like chewing on plastic, like pens. So you may be thinking that's a bit much, but kids do stuff like that, right? He would also chew on erasers, he'd chew on the TV remote buttons. Okay! That is a bit much but he was and still is today, extremely smart. We opted not to put Cody on the medication that the school psychologist recommended. I did however buy some vitamins and told him that it was the medication that would help him calm down and be able to pay attention in class. It actually seemed to be working for two weeks.

My husband came to visit me at work and brought Cody with him. It was a beautiful day outside and we'd decided to eat our lunch on the patio. Cody had finished his lunch and began to do backflips right there on the patio where we and others were having our lunch. His behavior was a bit odd, especially since he was in high school and a growing young man, but I still didn't believe at that time medication was necessary or the answer.

Cody is my second born. Growing up, he was a happy, vibrant child who from the age of about three-years-old, moved to the beat of his own drum. He loved to take things apart and put them back together and usually they were better off when he did. He was a seeker. He'd go looking for new things to discover. He loved learning and to that end, he read everything he got his hands on; newspapers, books, the dictionary, even the back of a cereal box. He was obsessed with learning new things and still is. Cody was fearless. I don't think that anything scared him.

I remember we moved into a brand new neighborhood. Most homes were still under construction, so it was a very quiet neighborhood with a huge field of weeds down the street from us. When you walked by, it was a bit eerie and uncomfortable. Cody was six-years-old at the time and he'd walk by that field all by himself. He'd be out playing with his older brother, Todd. As it would turn out, Todd would be ready to go home but Cody would want to stay a bit longer and play with his friends. Todd wouldn't argue or make him come along. He'd leave Cody and he'd come home and tell me that I had to go and retrieve his little brother because he'd refused to come home with him. I'd find my little Cody strolling along like he'd owned the place. No fear, no cares, or a worry in the world. Cody was a mama's boy for sure. Todd was my first and a very independent child from the word go but Cody seemed to always need to know that I was there or very nearby. If I was leaving the house, he was coming with me, or at least he tried to come. I think this had a lot to do with his father and me divorcing. He wanted to make sure that I was not going to leave him too. Cody has always been a person who speaks his mind no matter what. He'd say, and still does, the things that most of us are thinking but too afraid to say out loud. That, in and of itself, is not a bad thing. Sometimes, however, it could be untimely and even hurtful. Cody's smile and laughter were both infectious and soothing. He made you feel that no matter what was going on, everything would be all right in the end. Cody has always been a protector of everything and everyone he loves. When he loves, he loves hard and forever. Cody was an ordinary child with some really extraordinary capabilities. I wouldn't have ever imagined that his life would have taken a much unexpected turn.

Like most parents, we have dreams, hopes, and plans for our beautiful, happy, perfect children, and they are sometimes abruptly interrupted by something that is completely out of our control. We never expected that there would be something like a mental illness in our story, in Cody's story. The class clown's smile began to turn upside down and that beautiful infectious smile eventually became a sad frown. The fire in Cody was flickering out and beginning to fade. It started with him accusing his teachers of being stupid. He said that they weren't teaching him anything that he didn't already know. Many people would tell me that perhaps he is just bored. That may have been true but he didn't have the passion and desire to learn as he once had.

We thought that perhaps it was growing pains. He was growing and getting older and some things were just changing. As time passed, Cody started testing the waters of rebellion a bit. He started cutting class here and there, becoming less and less interested in school. Like most parents, we had rules. Cody did not like the house rules. Bedtime was at 10 pm for him and that meant he had to be off the phone at 10 pm as well. Cody would sneak the phone in his bedroom and talk until the early morning hours. He didn't participate in doing any of his chores. At this point, we thought that he was just acting out. As I always say, one thing leads to another and there is usually an escalation. This was no different. Cody's bad behavior just got worse and worse. We thought perhaps he missed his father and we should allow him to go back to Los Angeles to live with his father. But things there were no better and Cody went to juvenile hall for the first time. I can't even begin to put in words as a mother what I felt at that moment. The heaviness in my heart was smothering me. The weakness I felt was crippling. I literally dropped to my knees and cried out to God, "Father, I stretch my hands to thee." There was no other name that I knew to call on other than the saving name of Jesus. Only Jesus could help us in this situation. I can honestly say that He heard me that day and He stepped in and turned that situation all the way around and I brought my baby back home. We were out of juvenile hall but far, far, far away from understanding what was going on with Cody.

It was another year and we were back in school and back on the football field. Cody had decided to turn the page and start a new chapter in his life. He seemed to be feeling good. I think that a short time in the juvenile hall was an eye-opener for him. We'd moved to a pretty affluent area because we wanted our children to attend better schools. He tried out for the football team and, just like everything else he put his mind to, he flourished, until a certain counselor decided that he needed to go to a continuation school to make up some missed credits and then come back to that school after having done so. As devastating as that was for me as his mother, it was a hundred times worse for Cody. The flame that seemed to be kindling in Cody, once again, had completely gone out. This was the beginning of an extremely tough road we'd take for the next few years. We had gone to the school board, brought in teachers and mentors to speak to the fact that Cody should not be placed in a continuation school. We begged and pleaded but they would not concede. Cody tried to make the best of it. For a short while, things seemed to go just okay.

Cody made lots of friends because of who he was. Everyone loved him. A good friend and nice young man that he befriended introduced him to MJ. I'm not talking about either of the Michaels-Jordan or Jackson; MJ as in Mary Jane, aka marijuana, pot, weed, or whatever it goes by these days. This was tough because Cody was starting to hang out late again, breaking curfew and even missing school more. I went to my local police department for help. I just wanted to make sure that he came home on time and that he went to school every day. I wanted also to try and get him into a program after school that would be motivating and that would keep him busy and focused on positive and productive activities. I was told that the only way that they could help me was if Cody was to break the law and get put into the system.

That had to be one of the most backward things I'd ever heard but that's exactly what was being told by the authorities. Now, remember, I mentioned that we had moved into an affluent area for better schools. Well, this was a predominantly white and very affluent neighborhood; the same neighborhood where the school Cody attended insisted he go to the continuation school across town and not the regular community high school that was right down the street from us. Are you following me? Keep that in mind and let's revisit it later...I needed help with Cody. My main objective was to keep my son safe. I called the authorities the next time he broke curfew and they actually took him to juvenile hall for breaking curfew. They quickly let him out but now he had gotten into the system and I thought that now they'd help me to help him, not even. Programs like the ones I'd read about like the young cadets and such were not available for those who were in the system. I was just beside myself but somehow I knew that it was going to be okay because God would surely make a way. I wished I had more time to tell you all the things that happened from that point on. I wish I could but let's just say, one thing definitely led to the next and things just escalated to the point that every one of us, me, my husband, our daughter, and our new baby boy, we were all affected in major ways. I never could have even imagined it but our lives were like Cody's smile, turned completely upside down.

I don't know about other mothers, but I never got used to seeing my child in handcuffs or sitting in a courtroom listening to a judge deciding the best sentence for a crime that my child had committed and in some cases, he did not commit. I wish that upon no one. I couldn't even believe that this had become our lives. I felt in my spirit that something else was going on with Cody. My child was not a criminal. He was not a bad person. He made a lot of bad choices, yes, but he wasn't bad. He had a heart of gold and I'd shared with him the things that were of The Lord all his life. I just couldn't figure it out; I didn't know what this was.

Cody would get these headaches from time to time which was likened to migraines. He would take aspirins and they'd eventually go away. I began to notice that the older he got, the worse the headaches got. I also noticed that the sadness that I'd seen in Cody was also getting worse. He would literally wake up very sad or sometimes very angry. You just didn't know what you were going to get from him daily. We were all kinda walking around on eggshells when he was around.

On one particular afternoon, Cody and I were sitting at the kitchen table; we were having a snack and a little conversation. I don't remember what the discussion was about in particular but I do remember he said to me, "Mom, you aren't listening to me. I'm so tired of feeling this way. I can't make it stop. Can you just make it stop?" At that moment I realized that all this time, I had not been listening. My approach had always been to fix things and do it quickly but this was something that was very unfamiliar, perhaps out of the range of my intelligence and it wasn't about me fixing it, it was about the fact that I was not listening. It wasn't my brain that Cody needed. He needed my heart. He needed me to hear him. I heard him tell me that he was hurt, he was scared and confused and he wanted it to stop. I wanted it to stop too. We all did.

About this time we would learn that my oldest son, Todd, who had gone into the military a few years before all of this, right out of high school, was diagnosed with Bipolar Syndrome (BPS). I admit that I'd heard of bipolar but really didn't understand what it was. I knew that it was a kind of mental illness but didn't understand what kind. Todd had come home from the military and seemed to be doing okay. He decided not to take medication because he said it made him feel like a zombie. He seemed to do well though without it. After hearing this news about Todd, I began to wonder could this be what was going on with Cody as well.

I became both fearful and confused. I wondered if both my boys could have a bipolar syndrome. I started to really pay close attention to Cody's behavior, studying his patterns, and moods. I read books on the matter, spoke with doctors and other experts. I wanted to reach out to friends, but who talks about mental illness? No one would dare admit that their child was struggling and especially not from a mental illness. That kind of talk would get you excommunicated from social circles. They don't even speak of it much in church. I told my husband of my thoughts and he just thought that Cody was a rebellious kid who consistently put his family through hell. Everyone believed that since Todd was diagnosed with BPS and was seemingly doing fine, Cody could do the same if he wanted to as well. I didn't believe that. Something was wrong and I was going to get to the bottom of it. I had to. I owed it to Cody, to our family.

I took Cody to our family doctor who gave him a head to toe physical. We talked a lot about Cody's medical history and background. We talked about the headaches too. Dr. Williams was especially interested in the headaches and felt that a lot of Cody's depression had come from the headaches. He said the physical pain can cause extreme depression and that Cody has been in pain for years and to that end, the pain had caused depression. I still asked if he felt that Cody could have Bipolar Syndrome given all that had transpired. He said that it was possible but first let's take care of the headaches and see what happens. We went home and Cody, being himself started researching everything about his headaches, when they started, how long they lasted, how they felt, where they're centered, etc.

We had an appointment with the neurologist so we went and Cody told him that he believed he had cluster headaches. Cluster headaches are far worse in comparison to migraine headaches. The doctor said, "If you were able to figure it out, you must be some kind of genius." After examining Cody and running some tests, he too diagnosed Cody with cluster headaches which can correlate with Bipolar Syndrome. He told Cody, "I guess you are in fact a genius." Cody went on to see a psychologist who formally diagnosed him with Bipolar Syndrome. We had it. We finally got our diagnosis. There was a method to all the madness. He wasn't a bad person, a criminal and I knew it.

Have you ever felt like as soon as you find out the name of what ails you, it just gets worse? Like, when you have these really strange feeling and you don't quite know what's going on and you soon find out that you are pregnant and that's why you had those feelings only to start feeling like ten times worse. Well, once we got the diagnosis, let's just say that stuff got real, real bad. The episodes were happening nonstop, back to back. My husband and I were struggling both individually and collectively. As quiet as it was kept, our marriage really began to struggle as well. Cody was older now. He was an adult but still living at home. He had become horribly rude and disruptive to our family and home. He was angry all of the time and it seemed my husband just wanted him out. He was the man of the house but Cody was constantly challenging him. He was so manipulative, pitching us against one another. I always felt like I was in the middle. I wanted and felt I needed to protect my son from himself and everyone who didn't understand that he was sick. That included my husband too. He didn't see Cody's behavior as a sickness at all. There were days that I felt we were not going to make it through. It was so intense. I started talking about it. I told friends, my church family, and anyone I thought might be able to help me. When I opened up about my Cody to friends, I quickly learned that many of my friends and their children were struggling too. I was amazed. I think my release liberated others. They felt comfortable with trusting me with their truths. My opening up about my son's illnesses was an act of obedience. I was laying my pride aside and for the first time allowing others to see the real me and what was going on inside me. It was the beginning of my healing and my freedom, though I didn't understand it then as I do now.

My church family unfortunately was not as welcoming. There were a few people, of course, those who were obviously going through it themselves, but not the leaders so much, which was largely disappointing. I spoke to many experts who lent me information, strategies, and techniques. I knew that this illness would be with both my boys for the rest of their lives but it didn't have to **be** their lives. This illness may not ever completely just go away but together we would learn how best to manage it successfully.

The Holy Spirit gives us all gifts, 1 Corinthians 12: 8-11 states, "For the one is given by the Spirit the word of wisdom; to another the word of knowledge by the same Spirit; To another faith by the same Spirit; to another the gifts of healing by the same Spirit; To another the working of miracles; to another prophecy; to another discerning of the spirits; to other divers kinds of tongues; to another the interpretation of tongues."

A similar thing can be said about healing when it comes to mental illness. To some, our Heavenly Father will heal with just a touch or a word. Oh yes, it has happened. To some, He will heal with continuous counseling and therapy, to another with medications, and another through the food and nutrition. We know that God has many ways to heal us but there are times when He doesn't.

Ask Paul, he said in 2 Corinthians 12: 7-9,

"And lest I should be exalted above measure through the abundance of the revelations there was given to me a thorn in the flesh, the messenger of Satan to buffet me, lest I should be exalted above measure. For this thing, I besought The Lord thrice, that it might depart from me. And said unto me, My grace is sufficient for thee: for My strength is made perfect in weakness."

So this is not something that would go away from my sons but God's grace is ever so sufficient, He has given them a way to live with this thorn and to manage it successfully. Cody's diagnosis is Bipolar with depression which he manages with food and diet and a daily routine that he does not part from. Todd was diagnosed with Bipolar with hypermedia and depression. Todd for the longest time would try and self-medicate as did Cody but Todd had initially decided not to take medication. After several failed attempts of suicide and living homeless from couch to couch with friends, he has finally succumbed to taking medications daily and they have helped him tremendously.

Though it is rarely discussed and is still lacking resources for many, especially in the African-

American community, mental illness is real and prevalent. It is infiltrating our children, families, our homes, and our lives. Know this though, we have a God who sits high and looks low. He sees all things, He knows all things, and in all things God works for the good of those who love Him, who have been called according to His purpose. It may seem like a travesty and maybe the hardest thing that you will ever encounter in your life. I implore you to look to the one who loves you, to trust in Him who can keep you and yours from falling. His grace is sufficient every day.

Chapter Reflection

"Thank you God for seeing our hearts. Our minds are so vulnerable and susceptible to every kind of evil. Our hearts are our lifeline. It's who we truly are."

Read and Meditate:

   Romans 12:2

   James 4:7

   2 Corinthians 10:3-5

   Proverbs 4:23

   Ephesians 6:16

Chapter 8

She Who the Son Has Set Free

"Be brave enough to believe you can be free from pain, shame, and guilt for the purpose of showing others what God can do in you when you're willing to yield to the process: It's worth the risk just as it would be if you were trusting a cardiologist with heart surgery!"
Leslie Arroyo

I am a bit older, a bit wiser, and a whole lot freer. I am no longer that little princess who was her daddy's shadow, following him around like a little puppy dog everywhere that he went and who sought after perfection and who chased after the "fine" boys. I finally found a way out of the deep dark tunnel, not by climbing up but I just kept going until I came upon a bend, I turned the corner and finally saw the light. My anxiety and panic attacks are very few and far in between these days and I no longer feel as if I'm going to die when they do happen. At this point, I think they are just hormonal. I've finally been able to grieve my babies, even the ones that I chose not to bring into this world. I've stood face to face and toe to toe with the spirits of abandonment and rejection that haunted me constantly, knowing now that I was never alone and I was chosen from the very beginning by the Most High God.

It's true sometimes, so many things happen to us in life and we feel that we will never make it through another day. Our burdens can be so very hard for us to bear that at times we just want to give up. There were certainly some heartaches and heartbreaks I experienced that caused me to pinch myself from time to time because I just knew the pain that I felt inside was going to kill me. But I thank God for His Son Jesus, our Savior. Jesus says this in Matthew 11:28-30, "Come to me, all you who are weary and burdened, and I will give you rest.

Take my yoke upon you and learn from me, for I am gentle and humble in heart, and you will find rest for your souls." We have heard and even read this scripture so often but we hardly ever do what Jesus asks us to do. Yet we say that we believe in Him and that we trust Him. We just won't listen to Him is all, I guess. I truly feel it's because we believe that things will just automatically change on their own, they'll just get better eventually. Maybe we believe it's easier to just suffer through it. Truth be told, there are a lot of things that Jesus asks us to do when we are in trouble and/or in need but we just won't do what it takes to get free or delivered from it. Is it that we are so comfortable in our shackles, that we don't seek freedom and deliverance, or do we not even realize that we are bound? For me, I think it may have been a little of both. I for once felt as I had earned and therefore deserved my shackles. I was kind of waiting for God to find me worthy of being free and the whole time He was just simply waiting for me to actually get to that point where I wanted to and was ready to be free.

I knew that Jesus didn't just leave His throne in Heaven, come down to earth, take on the form of man, lay down His deity, endure all that He endured including being lied on, talked about, mocked, beaten, and crucified on an old rugged cross just for me to be, okay. No. My Bible tells me in fact that He came so I might have life and have it abundantly. He came to save me and to reconcile me back to The

Father so that I may have a relationship with Him and He came to set the captives free. I didn't just want to be okay. I wanted to be free and I was going to be. Like Hannah I was tired. Hannah was a certain woman in the Bible who was barren. She was unable to have a child. Her womb was closed shut. Her husband's second wife was having children for him and she would taunt Hannah tirelessly. Hannah grew very weary and tired of the second wife being blessed with all of these children and Hannah had none. She felt empty and defeated. I think she may have even gotten angry a little bit with God and Hannah cried out and prayed to her God. Hannah prayed in such a way that the priest in the church thought she was drunk. She prayed desperately.

Have you ever been there? Have you ever been so tired and angry and you cried out to The Lord? Have you ever prayed desperately? I sure have. I wanted to know more about God. I wanted to heal; I needed healing of not just my body but my mind and spirit too. I was so downtrodden. You might be thinking but you said you were "okay." I appeared okay. I spoke like someone who was "okay" and my performance was, you know, "okay."

All around me folks were experiencing God on a level that I couldn't seem to attain. They seemed to have joy and a peace that was not of this world. There was this connection with The Lord that I desperately wanted and needed in my life. I wanted to tap in but I just couldn't seem to penetrate it. It seemed as if like Hannah, I was on the outside looking in.

It seemed so close but yet so far away and if they could have it, why not me, why not me, Lord? I prayed and I cried out to The Lord, Lord please deliver me, give me freedom, give me your peace. I told Him that I wanted more and more of Him. I told Him that I wanted to love as He loved and I wanted to forgive as He forgives. I wanted His heart. I realized to have what I saw others with, I needed to surrender some things that I was holding on to. If I wanted to be free I needed to relinquish the things that kept me bound. In theory that makes a whole lot of sense. In theory, it does. In reality, it's just not that easy but when you want it as bad as I did, you'll pray your way through like Hannah did and as did I.

There's a process when going through freedom and deliverance. Oh yeah! There is such a thing as going through freedom and deliverance where you will begin to shed or take off everything that has you bound, those things that you are aware of and those of which you are not. So the Holy Spirit led me right to it. I prayed for freedom and the Holy Spirit took my prayer to Jesus and put His translation on it and the next thing I know, I'm sitting with a minister of my church at the time, telling her things about myself I vowed never to tell another human being. Seriously friends, even as I was walking into the room to meet her, I had a conversation with myself and told myself exactly what I would and would not discuss in this meeting. I never shall forget, she asked me one question. I opened my mouth and my entire life fell right out of my mouth. Has that ever happened to you or have you ever had an out of body experience whereby you are speaking and you knew that you were going to say something that you shouldn't say and you couldn't stop yourself from saying it? It was like you were looking at yourself and you were screaming at yourself saying, "Don't say it, don't say it," but your mouth was no longer connected to your brain and so of course, you said, all of it. That's exactly what happened to me.

Initially, I was like, what did I just say? Why did I tell her all of those things? After a very short while that feeling passed away and I felt so much lighter, my spirit felt a certain peace. I remember a mentor of mine once told me, "We have not because we ask not." I wanted to heal. I had felt sick and in bondage for years. I feel like these chains had not been broken because I'd never asked God to break them. But He needed something from me as well. He needed me to surrender my fear of talking about my pain and where it came from. That would be the beginning of my freedom. So it didn't stop there. Next came the hardest part. I was asked to write down everyone that I felt I needed to forgive. Everyone that I was so angry with, that I resented and who had hurt me. To my surprise, that list was really long. There were names of those who I thought I'd forgiven but I realized I really hadn't. I was also asked to write down a list of people who I needed to ask for their forgiveness, those that I had wronged, hurt, or offended. Hmmm. That list was even longer, friends. The whole experience in and of itself was so humbling. My paper was filled. After the writing assignment, there was a time scheduled for me to come and meet with two of the ministers who would pray with me and petition The Lord for freedom and deliverance for me. I had no idea what this was going to look like. I tried asking a friend before time who had also gone through this process and all she could tell me was that it was life-changing and that I was going to feel so different afterward. Well, I was definitely hoping for life-changing but I had no idea what feeling different meant or would look like.

The day came and I was a bit apprehensive of course. The devil started with his same ole' tactics. I swear he does not have any new material. He will always use the same old things. He gets in your head and starts telling those same lies. He's always trying to convince me that God doesn't love me and that He won't do anything for me because I've sinned way too much for Him to bless me. He thinks if it worked so well once, it'll work again, and for the most part, it does, right? But not that time Devil. I was determined to get what The Lord had for me. I was going to be delivered and set free, period.

I arrived at the church and met the ministers at one of the prayer offices and so it began. The ministers asked for my list. They took some time to read over it and then began to pray and invite the presence of The Lord to enter into the room. I was still feeling some kind of way. I guess you could say it was a bit of fear of the unknown. I didn't know what was going to come next, what would happen. I began to pray with the ministers and one by one they began to pray that The Lord would open my heart and that He'd allow me to forgive each one as He forgives and has forgiven me. Likewise, they prayed, for each person, that I should seek to be forgiven, that I would repent and ask for God to forgive me for the sins and the offenses that I'd committed against others, each one on my list. As we all prayed and surrendered ourselves completely to Him, I could feel the presence of The Lord enter in. His presence filled the room as I'd never felt before. I should mention that for months before this I'd been suffering from vertigo. My equilibrium had been way off to the point I'd sometimes have to hold on to things when I was walking to keep my balance. Well, while we were praying together and I began to repent for my sins, my fears and doubts, all the resentment and bitterness and all the anger, as I cried my nose began to drain profusely. It wouldn't stop. It was like a clear mucus. I must have used at least three whole boxes of Kleenex, honestly. My nose just kept running and we all just kept praying and these two ministers began to pray about the actual circumstances connected to the names on my list and I was stunned because how did they even know what had happened when I'd only written down names. There was no way they could have known. I talked about many things in my first meeting but nothing directly connected to those specific names. That was the day that I met I The Holy Spirit.

Acts 1:8 tells us, "But you will receive power when The Holy Spirit has come upon you." I knew that The Holy Spirit had come upon them as they prayed for me. That was the only way they could have known this. Also in Isaiah 11:2 it says this, "And the Spirit of the Lord shall rest upon him, the Spirit of wisdom and understanding, the Spirit of counsel and might, the spirit of knowledge and the fear of the Lord." Y'all, I'm not making this stuff up. It's right there written in The Bible, the Word of God. A fear came over me but it wasn't the same fear that I usually had. This was the fear, the tremble, and an abundance of adoration for The Lord God Almighty. I wanted to be healed and free from bondage and He was releasing me as I completely submitted my whole life, everything, all of it, to Him. I could feel the chains breaking off of me. I could hear Him speaking directly to me. It was like nothing I'd ever experienced before. It was beautiful, amazing, and powerful and yes, it was life-changing. Needless to say when we were done my nose stopped draining, but I remember walking out of the church and I was standing straight up. I didn't have to hold onto anything to keep my balance. I didn't feel light-headed at all. There were no symptoms of vertigo. I felt like a feather floating with the breeze. Jesus didn't tell me afterward to go and tell anyone about the miracle that had just taken place but I just did. I immediately ran home and called everyone that I could think of who had not gone through this process of freedom and deliverance to do it right away. I told them my story. I told them that if they did this their lives would never be the same, that they'd be, as I was, set free.

I found freedom. Free at last, free at last, thank God Almighty, I'm free at last. I know that I described an event to you that had taken place in my life. Truth is that it wasn't just another event. It became my lifestyle. Every day that I wake up, I choose to be free. I choose to die to my flesh daily and walk in the Spirit. Being free is not a one-time deal. It's a choice that you must make always. The Devil, if nothing else, is relentless. He never stops coming for us. We can never stop seeking God, ever. We can't stop praying, reading God's Words, worshipping, and choosing life, choosing to be free. The Word of God says in John 8:36, "So if the Son sets you free, you will be free indeed." The Son has surely set me free. It goes on to say in John 14:6, "Jesus said to him, I am the way, and the truth and the life. No one comes to the Father except through me." Jesus tells us who He is in this verse and in John 8:32 He tells us this, "And you will know the truth and the truth shall set you free."

This is how I see if for those of us who have a desire to be delivered out of bondage and to be free in Christ Jesus. Come to know the truth, which is Jesus. Choose life, which is Jesus. Give everything to Him. I mean complete and total surrender. Surrender every fear, all of your cares, worries, unforgiveness, bitterness, hurt, sickness, whatever it is that keeps you in bondage and keeps you from living the abundant life that Jesus died for you to have, lay it all down. Let it go and you may need to do this every single day and that's okay. Let Him set you free. I promise, no matter what the Devil says, you will be free indeed.

Chapter Reflection

"Freedom usually comes with a price that most cannot pay. I am free and Jesus picked up the tab."

Read and Meditate:

2 Corinthians 3:17

Galatians 5:1, 13-14

Psalms 118:5

Acts 13:38-39

Chapter 9

Daily Prayer

"So if The Son sets you free, you are truly free."
John 8:36 NLT

Father, thank you for sending Your Son, Jesus down from Heaven to earth to set the captives free. Thank you that He died that we may have life and live abundantly. Father no matter how we started in life or where life may have taken us, we can still have freedom because Christ paid the price on the cross and He has made us free. Jesus, your redeeming grace opens the doors that were once shut and that kept us bound and it calls us into the freedom of your love. Lord, we ask that you forgive us for our transgressions and shortcomings. Forgive us for those times when we did not trust in You and the power of Your mighty, awesome, and life-changing Words. We praise you today Lord, for pulling us out of the darkness and being patient with us as we become accustomed to Your marvelous light. We thank you that you have set us free and that we are free indeed. Amen.

Chapter 10

I AM Who He Says I AM

"As you think and speak about yourself and others, consider this... Our Heavenly Father has never thought or spoken a negative word about you. Be as kind to His creation in thought and word as He has been to you." – Sharon E.

I've always considered myself to be pretty tough. I didn't think the way some people treated me really affected me. I believed some of the really cruel and mean things, folks, at times, would say to me or about me really didn't bother me, but boy was I wrong. I was affected, and rather deeply I might add. I remember I had this one aunt who would say things like, "You can't do the things that the other children do because you have a heart condition, and you are sickly." I was born with a heart murmur which I had grown out of by the age of ten. I'd gone to the doctor and he told Mama that it was gone, it just wasn't there anymore. Mama was confused because it had always been there since my birth and, now, just like that, it was gone.

My aunt would act as though it was still there and actually not allow me to participate in fun activities with her children because, in her words, I was "fragile." When she'd say it, it was almost like she was deliberately taunting me. She seemed to enjoy it. It was strange. She'd say it and then her children started saying it and before long others joined in and everyone would consider me to be a sickly and fragile child. After a while, I even believed it. I guess what they say is true; if you are called something long enough, you eventually begin to believe it. I believed that I was and even to this very day sometimes I still feel at times that I am fragile and think that I'm sick. I think the correct term for this is hypochondriac.

Yes, I wore the crown of strange illnesses for years. We don't realize the power of our words. Words can heal you or words can kill you. Just look at Proverbs 12:18 as it says, "The words of the reckless pierce like swords, but the tongue of the wise brings healing."

My daddy and mama had divorced but the most interesting thing happened. When they were no longer together as husband and wife, they became the best of friends, so much so that people would tell them that they should just get back together. They seemed to like each other a whole lot more than when they were married. I even said to Daddy, "Daddy, why don't you just move back home?" Daddy grinned and told me he couldn't do that. He knew that things were much better now between him and Mama and he said that he loved Mama and he always would but he could never live with her again. I was still much too young to understand these things. Daddy said that my mama had said some things to him that he could not put behind him and he would never forget them. He warned me right then to always mind my words. He said that sticks and stones may break your bones and words can and will most certainly hurt you. Boy was he right. No matter how good things are, how much fun you are having, or even how happy you are in the moment, you may not remember all the good times or the good things that happen in your life but you will remember every bad word spoken to you, over you and about you. You will never forget those words or how they made you feel and you may never truly know or understand the true ramifications or the depth of the assault that was inflicted upon you.

I remember hearing the people that I love the most say things to me that seemed relatively harmless. They'd say things like, "You are so scary, too fearful." Some would even say things like, "You are way too skinny, too spoiled, stuck up." They'd even tease me because I was a virgin. Can you believe that? I was talked about for being a virgin. I was called a prude, too religious. My sister would call me old fashioned and boring. She would tell me that I was just like my mama, in other words, I was old fashioned and I was no fun. Perhaps, this may seem quite silly to some of you, but those words had such a profound impact on my life. I became afraid of almost everything, including my shadow. I was afraid of the dark, afraid of being alone, afraid of people. I was afraid of living and terrified of dying. I became extremely self-conscious, especially my body. There were negative talk and criticism all around me. I'd like to be able to tell you that I just let it roll off my back like water off a duck, but when you are young, the things people say and their opinions of you do affect how you begin to see yourself. They often shape who you will become.

The truth is my daddy had spoiled me and he was so proud of it too. Yes, he gave me the sun and the moon. Though they made it seem as such, it was not a bad thing at all. He spoiled me mostly with his love. It seemed as if my forehead had been adorned with the letter "S" for spoiled and that seemed to be something terrible to some. Even being a virgin seemed as if it was a bad thing, at least it did back then.

I can tell you for sure that the pressure felt from being labeled as a virgin caused many of us, young girls, to give away our virginity a lot sooner than we would have liked to. These days, perhaps these things are really not a big deal but these were actual word curses that were constantly spoken over me for quite some time. I didn't realize it so much then, but these and so many other words that were spoken about me or to me would begin to shape who I'd become, what I'd believe about myself, my circumstances, my destiny, and how I would see others. It's true. Words are powerful. The Bible says in Proverbs 18:21, "Death and life are in the power of the tongue, and those who love it will eat its fruit."

What has been spoken over your life? What labels do you carry? Believe me, we have all had our fair share. I don't think that folks just intentionally say things to destroy you but it happens, right? Now, sometimes it is intentional, we know this, but mostly I think that people are completely unaware of the harm they are perpetuating and they don't seem to understand that there are consequences often connected to words that they speak. Consequently, we are guilty of this too.

I believe that when we don't truly know and understand who we are, who we belong to, and how much He loves each one of us or how He sees us, we will live in this space of believing every lie of the enemy. Even, we ourselves speak those same lies from the enemy to one another, to our children, to our children's children, and their children. I was sinking so deep, I became consumed with the lies. I not only believed them, I was convinced by them. Some of you may be as well. I was convinced that I was the worse person living because I had had an abortion. I was convinced that I was not good enough because my daddy left me. I was convinced that I wasn't smart enough; I was sickly and going to die. I was convinced that I was boring and old-fashioned, I didn't deserve to be happy because I had committed way too many sins. I walked around with this dark cloud over my head convinced that God didn't love me. He couldn't love someone like me. I was convinced that I wouldn't have a successful marriage because my mama's marriages didn't seem to work out. I could really go on and on. Now, some of these things were told to me by others, for whatever their reasons were, but if I'm honest, there are some things that I created in my mind because I'd become conditioned to the lies and all of the negativity.

I was constantly on this negative loop. I could not produce a positive thought to save my life. Some of my thoughts were worse than the things that had been spoken over me by others. I developed some seriously stinking thinking. Have you ever been there? Nothing good came my way. I was doomed. I was not going to amount to anything. I wouldn't get a degree, I would never purchase a home, my children wouldn't be anything. No man would ever truly want me, love me, I would never get that job or that position, I'd never write the book. The loop just played on and on. I even convinced myself that God hated me. Can y'all imagine that?

Some of you may find yourself here as well. I bet some of you have convinced yourselves of the same thing. You have probably heard some of the same word curses that I have and have convinced yourself of even worse things. Some of you are convinced that you'll never have a child, a husband. You don't believe you are smart enough to get the degree, poised enough to be a part of that organization, eloquent enough to speak on that stage speaking to those people, you aren't creative enough, not strong enough, not...enough. I'm telling you that it's all lies. Lies...I tell you.

It's a setup and a design from the enemy himself. He doesn't want you to know who God is because if you don't know who He is then you won't ever know who you are. If you don't know how much God loves you and what He thinks about you then you will never learn to love yourself and you will fall prey to the Devil himself, and if he then convinces you that you are nothing and that you are worthless or insignificant, then he is advancing his kingdom and his agenda. I need you to get this. This is why he never tires and he is always haunting you and taunting your mind. Look, the word of God tells us in John 10:10, "The thief comes only to steal and kill and destroy." He wants to steal your identity and your inheritance, kill your hopes and dreams of being all that you can be, and going as far as you can in this life and ultimately destroy your future, any chance of you obtaining salvation and advancing the Kingdom of God. Now is it starting to make sense to you?

Oh but God!!! Somebody just put praise right there. John 14:1 would say, "Let not your hearts be troubled. Believe in God: believe also in me." Thank you, Jesus. I thought I knew God. I thought because I had been in church for 40 something odd years that I knew God. Well, I knew of God. I knew what Mama and others said about God and who He was. I knew the story of Jesus Christ, the baby in the manger, and how He walked the earth for 33 years, and He was crucified but rose again on the 3rd day. Yes, I knew of Jesus, I thought.

You don't know anything until you have had

your experience. You have to read the Bible yourself. You have to pray for yourself. You have to get to know God, the Father, the Son, and the Holy Spirit for yourself. Then and only then will you truly know our God. It's called a personal relationship. It's intimate. When someone says that you don't know Him like I do, believe them because you don't. My relationship is going to be different from yours, the same God, different experiences. I said to myself that there had to be more to God than what others were telling me. How come they seem to know Him so well but me not so much? I committed to knowing Him. I told Him that I wanted to know Him. Of course, I prayed because that's just what I do. I sought Him early in the morning and searched for Him all day, every day. I said, "Lord reveal yourself to me." He answered and He led me to a church and from the moment I walked through that first Sunday, I began to actually see Him. I was quite serious.

I dug my heels in and I began to go deeper and deeper. He would reveal Himself to me in certain situations and experiences, But when He led me to His Word, that's where it all changed. God is illuminated in His Words. Since we are all about technology these days, I Googled, "Who does the Bible say that God is?" I chose 30 passages of scripture that would tell me who God is. I put a scripture every day on the calendar and I'd read a scripture a day. I'd meditate on it day and night.

One of my favorites was found in Exodus 3:14, "I am that I am; He said, Thus shalt thou say unto the children of Israel, I am hath sent you." Wow, my God is a straight-up boss, right? Honestly, friends, God is amazing. He is the creator of all things and there is not a single thing that He did not create. He is omnipotent which means He has unlimited power. He can do anything. He is omniscient. He knows all things. He is the sovereign of the sovereign. God Spirit Father, The Son and The Holy Spirit are individual yet indivisible.

They are all the same God. I tell you this; please study your Bible, the living Word of God. Come to know your creator, your redeemer, healer, provider, and your protector, strong tower, your true friend, your very best friend, your comfort in times of sorrow, the lamb that was slain, the one who is the light of the world. He's the Prince of Peace, the wheel in the middle of a wheel, Savior of the world, the one who loves you, He who himself is love. He is the King of Kings, The Lord of Lord, the Alpha and Omega, He who was and is and is to come. He is God and God all by Himself but don't just take my word for it. Read it and study it for yourself. Seek Him and you will find Him, believe that.

Psalms 139:14, "I will praise thee; for I am fearfully and wonderfully made; marvelous are thy works; and that my soul knoweth well." David reminds us that we are God's masterpiece. He fashioned us. He's always loved us and because He loved us so well He created us in His own image. He sent His Son to die for our sins that we could be in a relationship with Him. The most read scripture in the Bible is one I mentioned earlier, it says it like this in John 3:16, "That God so loved the world, that He gave His only begotten Son, that whosoever believeth in Him should not perish but have everlasting life." He even goes a bit further to explain His love for us in Romans 5:8, "But God demonstrates His own love for us in this: while we were still sinners, Christ died for us." Just let that sink in for a moment. Not when we got our act together, not when we decided to turn to Him and love Him but He loved us from the very beginning, while we were still in our mess, hot mess.

The enemy does not want you to know God for this very reason. When you start knowing God, you start growing in God and when you start growing in God, you start going with God. You start to be convinced of who He is and who He says that you are in Him. You start being convinced that you are enough, you are beautiful in the sight of God, and that He believes you are worth dying for. You are the redeemed of The Lord, you are chosen, you are a miracle, and you are a citizen of the Kingdom and an heir to the throne of Christ. These life-giving sentiments don't even begin to scratch the surface of who He says that you are. Get into it. God says, you are holy, a new creature, justified, loved and you are healed, you are free. Also know that you are delivered, accepted and you, my friend, Are complete. You are an overcomer, a conqueror and you are triumphant. Get to know Him, I encourage you. Know how much He loves you and just how much you mean to Him. This is how you silence the noise of the enemy. This is what keeps you focused on the kingdom and this my beloveds is how we win. There's a song out there that says, "He knows my name." He knows your name, the name that He gave you before the foundation of the earth. You need to know your name. He calls you the righteousness of God, the head and not the tail, the lender, and not the borrower. He calls you alive, His friend, His child, and He calls you loved. He says that you are His own.

Understand that you may do some things that you are not proud of. You may make some mistakes along the way. To some, you may not be the prettiest, strongest, or the brightest apple in the basket. Your family may have gone through hell and back. Today you may not have the house, the car, or the fanciest clothes but understand me good, okay; none of that matters. God created you on purpose and with purpose. You are the apple of His eye. You are living for the approval of one and that is your God. What anyone else says or thinks is none of your business. Your business is The Kingdom of God.

The Bible tells us to do this in Philippians 4:8, "Finally, brethren, whatsoever things are true, whatsoever things are honest, whatsoever things are just, whatsoever things are pure, whatsoever things are lovely, whatsoever things are of good report; if there be any virtue, and if there be any praise, think on these things." For me, those things spoken in Philippians 4:8 are the things of God, so for me, having come to know my God and knowing myself in Him and discovering His matchless love for me, I am utterly convinced that I am exactly who He says I am and there's not a thing I or anyone else can do about it.

Chapter Reflection

"Branded with His name, Child of God."

Read and Meditate:

Isaiah 43:1

John 1:12

John 15:15

Romans 8:17

Romans 8:2

2 Corinthians 5:17

Ephesians 1:3

1 Corinthians 1:30

Chapter 11

Walk it Out Everyday

"Leaving behind something familiar can be challenging. However, it gets easier when you walk towards what's unfamiliar. Why? Because you've empowered yourself by making the decision to move forward. It's never as hard as you think."
Tina Marie

Since the very beginning of time, we were given a choice to choose from the Tree of Life or the Tree of the Knowledge of Good and Evil. Choosing between these two would ultimately dictate our approach and response to God and would further have a profound effect on the choices we'd make for the rest of our lives. In Genesis 2:16-17, God says to Adam, "You may freely eat the fruit of every tree in the garden except the Tree of the Knowledge of Good and Evil. If you eat its fruit, you are sure to die." He was not demanding that Adam not eat the fruit from the Tree of the Knowledge of Good and Evil but He wanted Adam to understand the ramifications of eating such fruit. God desires for us to live and not die. The death He was speaking of was not just physical death but spiritual death which is far worse. This choice between the Tree of Life and the Tree of the Knowledge of Good and Evil was not just an event that took place with Adam and Eve in Genesis but this is the choice that we have today, every day, and in everything that we do.

Every day we must decide which tree we are going to choose from. Will we choose life or will we choose death? This must be your lifestyle, not an event. As I've said many times throughout this book, the enemy, or if you choose to call him the Devil, does not sleep, take a vacation, or even a short 15-minute break. He is relentless and he will stop at nothing to steal from you, try to kill you, or get you to kill yourself and to ultimately destroy you and what God has placed on the inside of you. Joshua 24:15 says, "And if it seem evil unto you to serve the Lord, choose you this day whom ye will serve; whether the gods which your fathers served that were on the other side of the flood, or the gods of the Amorites, in whose land ye dwell: but as for me and my house, we will serve the Lord."

My hope is that you will choose every single day from the Tree of Life, choosing Jesus because Jesus is life. The fruits from the Tree of Life are life-giving, life-changing, and lifesaving. They are the fruits of the Spirit as in Galatians 5:22-23, "The fruit of the Spirit is love, joy, peace, forbearance, kindness, goodness, faithfulness, gentleness, and self-control. Against such things, there is no law." When I speak of our approach to God and our response to Him, I'm speaking about knowing for ourselves, who He is, and always has been from the very beginning. I don't know about you but for me growing up in a Baptist Church, I learned a great deal about God, mostly that He would get me if I messed up and that I would go to Hell. Now whereas there is such a thing as hell, our God is a God of love, in fact, He is love. He loves us so much and has since before creation. His desire is for us to live, to be free, to have a relationship with Him, and to accept His son Jesus. He embodies the fruits of the Spirit. That is what He wants for our lives. All we have to do to obtain these things is to choose them every single day.

You are probably thinking to yourself that it's a lot easier said than done, choosing life every day and in every situation. I don't disagree with you there. Sometimes it's not easy at all and sometimes it seems utterly impossible but it's not easy living a life filled with hatred, bitterness, anguish, impatience, unkindness, wickedness, inaccuracy, brutality, or lack of discipline. The list goes on and on, right? Let's be honest. We've seen what happens when we just rely on ourselves, leaning on our understanding, and doing whatever it is we want to do. We think because we are saved, we've been baptized, oh, and, of course, because we go to church every other Sunday, we can just live life however we want and we do just that. Usually, we are not choosing from the Tree of Life when we do.

Choosing from the Tree of Life takes a conscious effort on our part. Choosing life is deliberate, friends. By nature, we are given to sin since the very fall of man. We have become enslaved by our flesh. Galatians 5:19-21 says this, "Now the works of the flesh are evident: sexual immorality, impurity, sensuality, idolatry, sorcery, enmity, strife, jealousy, fits of anger, rivalries, dissensions, divisions, envy, drunkenness, orgies, and things like these."

Do any of these things sound familiar? I'm just going to go ahead and be completely transparent here. I've subscribed to many of these things and more often than not, I chose it. But I thank God for Galatians 2:20,

"I have been crucified with Christ. It is no longer I who live, but Christ who lives in me. The life I now live in the flesh, I live by faith in the Son of God, who loved me and gave himself for me."

And even in this I wake up every day and die to my flesh and choose to live by choosing from the Tree of Life. I have to... You have to... We have to be intentional about this thing. We have to be as relentless as the enemy and we have to be determined to live and not die physically, mentally, financially, emotionally, and definitely not die spiritually. You may not hit the mark every single time but if making the choice daily becomes your actual lifestyle and not just a one-time event, you'll get pretty darn close. Do your part, make the choice...every day and let our God do the rest. I promise you, He won't let you down. Our God never fails us. Romans 10:12 says, "For whoever believes in Him will not be disappointed. This includes everyone."

I'm guessing that most have heard the expression, "Don't just talk the talk, walk the walk," right? Well, that's what we have to do. We have to walk this thing out. I know you are wondering what does that mean? I'm glad you asked. This is what it looks like. First and foremost, we must seek The

Lord at all times. Matthew says in chapter 6 verse 33, "But seek ye first the kingdom of God, and his righteousness; and all these things shall be added unto you." How many things will be added unto you? All things will be added unto you. Some folks will say don't take the Bible so literally. Well, I believe everything that the Word of God says and I suggest that you do too. Seek Him every day and seek Him in all things.

Next, Jesus says in John 15:4, "Abide in Me, and I in you. As the branch cannot bear fruit of itself unless it abides in The Vine, so neither can you unless you abide in me." We have to abide in The Lord and He will also abide in us. It's the perfect exchange. We should spend time in communion with The Lord, building a relationship with Him. This is His heart's desire. This is why Jesus came so that we could have a relationship with the Father. He wants us to abide in Him because that's how we can connect with Him and become one with Him. The connection with Him is mutual, reciprocal. Also, the vine gives life to the branch, and Jesus who is the Vine gives life to us. Abiding in Him also implies that we need to depend solely on Him, not on ourselves or others but our Lord. This is not reciprocal because obviously, He does not need to depend on us for anything, right? But we who are the branch need the vine for its very survival. The branch is powerless without it. The vine provides everything that the branch needs to grow and to produce fruit. To me, this seems like the perfect reason for us to abide in The Lord. To take this thing even a bit further, the word "abide," in Greek means to remain or to stay with.

Another way in which we walk out our faith is to stay with Jesus. It's not just for an event or a season but life. Remember, this has to become our lifestyle. The disciples asked in John 1:38-39, "Turning around, Jesus saw them following and asked, What do you want? They said, Rabbi (which means Teacher), "where are you staying?" "Come," he replied, 'and you will see." So they went and saw where he was staying, and they spent that day with him. It was about four in the afternoon. Now we could certainly argue that it was easier for the disciples because they actually had Jesus there with them every day and they had easier access to Him. Believe me, I hear you but we have our faith in God and we have The Word of God. Some of you may be sucking your lips and rolling your eyes at me right now but let me say this to you, I dare you to work your faith, just exercise it a bit. When I say a bit y'all, that's what I mean. In fact, you need even less than a bit. The Bible tells us in Matthew 17:20, "Truly I tell you, if you have faith as small as a mustard seed, you can say to this mountain, Move from here to there, and it will move. Nothing will be impossible for you." If you don't believe it then perhaps it could be it's because you have never tried it, just a little food for thought. In my times of trouble, worry and distress, I got to the place where I would just say, "Lord, I'm giving this over to you because I've done all that I can in my own strength." I'd release it all to Him who can keep me from falling and He has always come through. I know it's scary but I truly encourage you to do it. As Steve Harvey says in his book, "Jump: Take the Leap of Faith to Achieve Your Life of Abundance." Either He will catch you when you fall or He will teach you how to fly." Either way, you win. The Word of God is everything, friends. Read it, speak it, eat it, digest it, sleep with it, wake up with it, live with it, and believe it.

It's sometimes hard to understand, I know, but The Holy Spirit reveals all things of God to us. It says so in 1 Corinthians 6:12, "What we have received is not the spirit of the world, but the Spirit who is from God, so that we may understand what God has freely given us." I didn't always understand everything in the Bible and truth be told, I still don't always understand initially but I pray and ask The Holy Spirit to reveal its meaning and He never fails me. I believe that He will do it and He does. It goes back to having that faith and simply believing. The point is to put your faith in God and stay in His Word every day or as much as you possibly can.

One thing I used to do was write my scriptures down on sticky notes and place them throughout the house where I could see them or put them down on index cards and keep them with me. Every chance I got, I'd read them over and over again. I studied His Words, meditated on them and they began to saturate my soul. They took residency in my heart. Now I'm not going to say that, like some folks, I can just rattle off all scriptures at all times. No, I'm not that person but when I need His Word because His Words live in my heart when I need them, The Holy Spirit brings them to my recollection every single time. His Words give me hope, guidance, inspiration, and correction. In fact, in Hebrews 4:12, The Word of God says, "For the word of God is living and active, sharper than any double-edged sword, piercing until it divides soul and spirit, joints and marrow, as it judges the thoughts and purposes of the heart." I really love the way that 2 Timothy puts it. It says in chapter 3:16-17, "Every scripture is inspired by God and useful for teaching, for reproof, for correction, and training in righteousness, that the person dedicated to God may be capable and equipped for every good work."

Why is this good news? I'm glad that you asked. Our Father is so amazing that He not only created us for Himself. Just let that part rest in your spirit. He chose you. He wanted you. He knew that we would sometimes have some difficulties in this life but He didn't just leave us to our own devices. No, no. He sent His Son to save us from sin and death. He allowed His Son to die on a cross for the cause. Now allow that to just marinate. When the job was done, the ransom was paid for us by Jesus, He left us His Word to help us navigate through this life here on earth and He even went a step further and left us His Spirit. He placed it inside of us. Are you understanding me? Lean into it y'all. Come closer. We are fully equipped and have every single thing that we need to overcome life's adversaries, all those fiery missiles that the enemy throws at us, the hopelessness, the despair, the bitterness, anger, fear, failed marriage, drug addiction, wayward child, loss of a loved one, mental and physical illnesses, and whatever else comes your way. The Word of God, work it, get into it, and walk this thing out.

Mama used to say, "Pray and pray without ever ceasing." I'd wake up many mornings and I'd find her on her knees praying and crying out to The Lord. That's back when people used to actually get on their knees and pray. Nowadays not many folks will get down on their knees and pray. We pray in bed, in the shower, or in our cars. It's okay, friends. Pray hanging from a tree, it really doesn't matter as long as you pray and pray without ceasing.

How do I pray? Well, I'm glad you asked. You can pray The Lord's Prayer in Matthew 6:9-13,

"Our Father in heaven, hallowed be your name, your kingdom come, your will be done, on earth as it is in heaven. Give us today our daily bread. And forgive us our debts as we also have forgiven our debtors. And lead us not into temptation, but deliver us from the evil one."

But really praying is just having a conversation with God. He's not a stranger. He's your Heavenly Father. He created you. He loves you and you love Him. Just simply talk with Him. Give Him thanksgiving and give Him praise for every day, for your life. Ask Him to forgive you for your sins daily. Tell Him your heart's desires and tell Him about your troubles. Ask The Holy Spirit to direct your path and lead you into all righteousness and petition to Him on behalf of others. Just talk to Him. I promise you this, that prayer moves the hand of God.

Walk it out with prayer. Remember again, this is not an event. This has to be your lifestyle. We do this every single day. It's not only that an apple a day keeps the doctor away. A prayer a day will help you slay. You don't have to take my word for it, try it and see for yourself, I dare you to do it. Another thing that I want you to do is to just begin praising God. Praise Him at all times. I am sure that you have heard it said, "Let everything that has breath praise ye The Lord." Praise The Lord. No matter what is going on in your life, give Him praise for all of it. King David was said to be a man after God's own heart for David had found favor with God. Now David was by no means perfect. He didn't always have it all together and the enemy was always coming for him because he knew David's potential. All odds seemingly were against David too, as you may feel at times that the world is against you, but David praised God without ceasing. You could always find David praising God. In fact, in Psalm 145 David says, "I will exalt you, my **God** the King; I will **praise** your name forever and ever. Every day I will **praise** you and extol your name forever and ever."

I suggest taking a few pages from David's book and give The Lord your worship and praise every single day for He is truly worthy of all the glory and all of your praise. You don't have to wait until church on Sunday. Praise Him every day, where you are. Miracles happen when we praise. Our praise is like a sweet aroma to his nostrils. Psalm 22:3 says, "He is enthroned in the praises of His people," and when we give Him the praise He is right there in the midst. He's with us.

I am by no means suggesting that by incorporating all these things in your life you will live a life free of troubles. Unfortunately, on this side of Heaven, such a thing does not exist, **but** God has made provision for us to be able to live on this side of Heaven and live life abundantly in Him. We can overcome, persevere, excel, be victorious, and we can win in this life. We can have the peace of God and joy that only comes from God.

We can have our hearts' desires. When the enemy rears his ugly head, we can stand up against him. The Word of God says clearly in Philippians 4:13, "I can do **all** things through Christ who strengthens me." So every day when you wake up, decide to choose the Tree of Life and simply live. Since this is not really about us and all about Jesus, we must make it our lifestyle to seek God and His Kingdom every day. We must rest and abide in The Savior, our vine, our lifeline. Like they used to say back in the day in the church I grew up in, "Watch, Fight and Pray," every day. Do you remember that? Pray in and out of season, it's literally a conversation with Him. I truly enjoy going about my day just talking to The Lord. He calls me a friend. I love talking to my friend, my true friend. It moves Him and blesses me.

I can't think of anything more satisfying than giving The Lord all of my praise every day. I praise Him for waking me up, for every blessing, protection, provision, the air I breathe, and for every beat of my heart, I give Him praise. I sing and we dance. I love dancing with The Father. This is how you walk out your faith. This is how you live a God-focused life. This is how you get free and stay free. This is how you overcome and be victorious. This is how you win. This is my story and I think I'm going to stick with it. God be with you always and bless you abundantly.

Chapter Reflection

"Life is such a beautiful journey. There are highs and lows, pitfalls and triumphs. Don't you dare stop. Walk it out for He who walks with you will protect you, hold your hand and carry you when needed."

Read and Meditate:

Psalms 119:45

Chapter 12

Dear God: A Letter from a 40-Year-Old Orphan

"Willing yourself to keep going, to believe when you don't seem to have a reason to, is a superpower women are born with. We keep going, despite the odds. We persevere. We persist. We are phoenixes that always find a way to rise."
Stacey Martz

DEAR GOD: A LETTER FROM A 40-YEAR-OLD ORPHAN

Heavenly Father, It's crazy the things that we take for granted; running water, electricity, a roof over our heads, and food on the table. We go about our lives just expecting to always have these things, expecting that in some way, somehow, they will always be available to us. I guess for many of us at least, we've never been without it, so no reason to even imagine not having it. Sometimes we even view people and our relationships the same way. They've always been there so we never imagine a world in which they don't exist. I made this very mistake myself.

Lord may I just take this opportunity to say, I'm so deeply sorry. When my daddy died I never even saw it coming. I never once in my life imagined that he would never be there. He'd even tell me things like, "Puss, I'm not always gonna be here," when he was trying to teach me something really important that would help me if something would happen to him. I'd learn the lesson sure, but I never thought that one day, my daddy would be gone. Lord, it truly never entered my mind. The words "death" and "daddy" did not coexist with one another in my head.

Father you know, my daddy and I were thick as thieves. We stuck together like glue. The sun rose and set on my daddy as far as I was concerned. I shall never forget one day when I called myself "being grown-up" and I actually got mad at Daddy because he'd taken my mama's side about something. Funny thing is, I don't even remember what that something was today. It was probably nothing at all. My feelings were hurt though and so being grown, I decided I was not going to call Daddy for a few days. Lord, you know that Daddy and I spoke nearly every day. It didn't matter where he was, he called me or I was certain to call him, so, us not speaking was hard. I wanted to talk to my daddy. I told him everything, he was my best friend in the world.

Mother's Day was coming up and a dear friend of mine gifted me with a weekend stay in a hotel. I was very grateful and I wanted to tell Daddy about it but I would need to call him to do that and I was busy proving a point. In hindsight, I was proving my own immaturity and selfishness. Believe me, this was one of the most expensive lessons I've ever had to learn. I'm certain this is the reason we are encouraged not to let the sun go down on our wrath with one another.

The day came for me to go on my weekend excursion. I wasn't as excited as I could have been because I missed him so. I arrived at the hotel and, as I was beginning to unpack, my phone rang. I thought, *who's calling me?* I didn't tell anyone what I was doing or where I'd be. I'd just spoken with my boys and they were safe and sound with their dads. Just as I thought to myself I wasn't going to answer,

I picked up and low and behold, it was my daddy. I had not been happier to hear from someone. Immediately I felt so remorseful for my awful behavior. I apologized to my daddy and I told him where I was and how a friend had gifted me with such a wonderful mini-vacation. He thought it was wonderful too and he reminded me about our Mother's Day tradition to have breakfast together and to go buy flowers and cards for all of the mothers in our immediate family. I promised Daddy that I would come over the next morning which was Mother's Day and we'd keep up with our tradition. He agreed that would be fine. Before hanging up the phone, I asked, "Daddy, would you like me to come over tonight and stay at your place with you?" He told me that tomorrow morning would be just fine.

Lord, I remember you woke me up about 11:45 that night. I felt as if I could not breathe. I didn't know why at the time but I could not go back to sleep. I just sat up all night long waiting for the sun to come up so that I could go and see my daddy. Lord what happened that next morning changed my life for the rest of my life. Daddy and I didn't have breakfast. We didn't get to purchase any Mother's Day cards for all the mothers in our circle. I didn't get to hear his voice or see his face with that infectious smile that day. It was as if tomorrow and Mother's Day never really came that year. My Daddy was gone.

My Lord, I know in the Bible Paul says in 1 Corinthians 15:55, "O death, where is your victory? O death, where is your sting?" On May 11th, 1996, death's sting was piercing my heart. It woke me up from a sound sleep and paralyzed my soul. The finality of death literally takes away your breath and rocks you to the very core of your being. No matter how loud the screams, the wrenching pleas and cries of disparity and pain cannot overturn or change what has been ordained and predestined from the very beginning of our existence. God, Father, you smiled upon me and showed me mercy. You quickened my spirit. I felt your presence with me and in me. You were moving through me. I remembered what Mama had told me. So, although my flesh wanted to ask so badly, I didn't ask you why. I trusted you.

As time went on and I grew older, I learned and later understood that every one of your creations has a purpose. My daddy was your creation too and he had served his purpose here on earth and you'd brought him home to be with you in Heaven. I still miss him with every sunrise but the memories of him and knowing that he is in Heaven with you carries me through. It gives me great joy. Though certain family members and friends too thought that I wasn't going to make it without him, you knew that I was going to be alright. They were all ready to see me fall. One of the world's most prolific authors and one of my most favorite human beings in the world once said, "Just like moons and like suns, With the certainty of tides, Just like hopes springing high, Still I'll rise," Maya Angelou, Still I Rise. And I did just that. It wasn't, hasn't been easy but you Lord, have been with me every step of the way and I thank you. Your Word says in Joshua 1:9, "Have I not commanded you? Be strong and courageous. Do not be frightened, and do not be dismayed, for the Lord your God is with you wherever you go."

The craziest, most unexpected thing happened after my daddy passed. I never saw this coming either. By now Lord you are probably thinking that I'm pretty clueless when it comes to a lot of things. You might be right. Of course, you are, you are God. It's kind of sad to say actually but, given how things had been going for most of my life, up until this point, there were no clues that this would ever come to pass. Mama and I became really close like best friends close. I know that this was You because there was just no way that this could ever be but, Father, I'm so grateful that it happened. I'd been waiting for Mama to see me, to hold me, to love me, and finally, she did. It was right on time. There was not even a period of catch up. We just connected instantly as if we'd always been. We laughed, we talked and talked all the time just like me and Daddy. She taught me things. She took an interest in me and the children. She stepped in right when I needed her the most and she became my new best friend in the world. Lord, I remember at one point feeling that I never wanted to be like my mama. You know 'cause Mama was a bit cold at times. Now I was experiencing my mama in a brand new way. She was amazing. I was so proud of her. I would be honored to be the woman of God, the mother and grandmother, the daughter, the sister, and friend that she was. Lord, I believe that you gave me a new pair of lenses to see her through and I began to see Mama the same way you saw her, as your beautiful masterpiece, your chosen, your child just like the rest of us.

3,707 days of my mama's love. Oh, how I had always longed and waited for it. Lord, I now know that my mama loved me from the moment I was conceived. She just didn't know how to fully express it and I grew to understand that, that was okay. In those ten years, we grew together in love, we grew together in you and your Word and we grew in our relationship with each other. I wouldn't have changed a single thing.

I saw my mama for my 40th birthday. I did not know that would be the last birthday of mine we'd celebrate together. Mama was fine, so I thought, but Mama was really very sick. Neither of us knew just how sick until it was too late. Mama had the worst cancer, I'm told, that there was. Her doctor told me that there was only a 7% survival rate and it was also the most painful. God, how great thou are. You did not let Mama suffer. The doctor said that my mama should have been in some immense pain but she wasn't. And Lord, you did not allow my mama to suffer long. Your mercy is sufficient and great is your faithfulness. Though I lost my best friend, yet again, I just want to say, thank you!

There is a scripture that says in Isaiah 26: 3, "**You keep** him in **perfect peace** whose mind is stayed on **you** because he trusts in **you**." My Lord you see, Mama and Daddy gave me many, many gifts but the most awesome gift of all was the gift of You. I was in the church with both my mama and my daddy from a baby learning about you and your only begotten Son. Daddy may not have been a good husband and he may have made more than his share of mistakes, but he took me to the house of prayer with him. I watched Daddy sing praises to you in the choir, saw him kneel, and pray in the front of the church on the deacon's row. I heard him call his Heavenly Father. Mama taught me to fight, watch and pray, and pray every single day. She taught me to hold on to God's unchanging hand and never let it go. My mama taught me how to provide shelter for the homeless, to clothe the naked, to feed the hungry, and to love everybody. Mama also taught me to read my Bible and my Bible told me in Proverbs 22: 6, "Train up a child in the way he should go: and when he is old, he will not depart from it." That's what my mama and my daddy did for me. Some folks think that scripture only applies to a child's behavior. You know, if you raise your child right, then he or she won't get into any trouble. Lord, for me it means a whole lot more because a child doesn't have to do anything bad to meet up with trouble because even when you are raised to do the right things and you are actually doing the right things, trouble can still meet with you and when that happens Mama and Daddy's training is going to be exactly what you need.

Trouble came for me on May 11th, 1996, and then trouble came for me again on June 29th, 2006. It wasn't the cause of death that brought the trouble rather it was the effects of death. Lord, you took my mama and my daddy home with you. I knew that they were home, that wasn't troubling for me. Trouble wanted me to give up. Trouble wanted me to lose my mind, to throw in the towel, to get high and drunk. Trouble tried to make me weak and keep me bound, to stop believing in God. But in the midst of all of that trouble, I could hear my daddy saying, "I got a feeling everything's going to be alright." And I could hear my mama saying, "Baby, trouble does not last always and joy, unspeakable joy comes in the morning." That's the training that saved me. That's the training that I would not, could not, and did not depart from.

So, Father, by the world's definition of an orphan, I had become one by the age of 40. I'd lost both my mama and my daddy. I felt and sometimes still do feel like a leper. I didn't have either of my grandparents from either side of my family. I'd also lost two of my children. Death had seemingly taken up residency in my life, in me. I had become consumed with it. I thought that people would treat me differently, feel pity for me. At times I feel incredibly lonely. I long for my mama and my daddy, especially when those around me are spending time with and celebrating their parents. But God, like I've said before and will always testify, just like in Psalm 46:1, "**God is our refuge and strength, a very present help in trouble.**" The reality is that there will be difficult **trouble and that's okay because I will always have you. Father, I love you and I thank you for always being right there by my side through it all.**

Love you always,
Your daughter,
Wandah

Chapter Reflection:

"The reality is that there will be difficult trouble and that's okay because I will always have you."

Read and Meditate:

Exodus 22: 22-24

John 14:18

Psalm 146:9

Chapter 13

An Attitude of Gratitude

*"Humility says thank you, giving back expresses appreciation. Acts of kindness comes from the heart, but, **gratitude** tops the chart!"*
Audra Jackson

My mom says, if you're good to people God will be good to you. I have so much gratitude in my heart for God's mercy and grace for He has been better than good to me!
LaWanna Bradford

Toda Roda in Hebrew means, "Thank you so much," and I thank every one of you who have joined me on this journey. This book has been a long time coming. I can honestly say that it cost me a lot of blood, sweat, and tears and then some! Today I can say it's okay. I understood at a point in my life that none of what I was going through was meant to destroy me or to take me out. It wasn't personal. Sometimes it can be hard not to believe that God isn't out to get you and that He is actually on your side. God wasn't out to get me. Everything, all of it was all about Jesus Christ and the building up of His Kingdom. When I thought God was hurting me, He was actually helping me. When I thought He didn't love me because of all the pain and suffering I was enduring, He actually had me on the potter's wheel spinning me into perfection. Not perfection as we understand perfection but the perfection He created me to be. He was going to make certain that I became exactly what he purposed for me to be and He's doing the same for you too. The Bible tells us in Philippians 1:6, "Being confident of this, that He who began a good work in you will perform it until the day of Jesus Christ."

Though at times I didn't think I'd actually make it through some of those very tough times, I thank God because He knew that I would. It was all a part of His perfect plan and will for my life. It was meant for me to come alongside those who were on a certain path that I myself had journeyed on before. I'd be able to tell them which road to take, how fast or slow to travel, what to take with them and what to leave behind, what to expect and those things they should absolutely stay away from. Most importantly, I'd be able to share with them how to reach their destination safe and sound. I could answer their questions and speak to their hardships and help them to face their mountains and even conquer their giants. It is indeed my honor.

As Paul once said, "I count it all joy." And then, ultimately, The Father would have me write a book, a personal memoir that would speak about my own trials and my struggles with fear, anxiety, distrust, abandonment, and a host of other things that caused such a deep sense of hopelessness and despair inside me. A book, however, that would also speak about how my love for and faith in God would ultimately lead me to an insatiable longing for being delivered from the pain and suffering and to live completely free in Jesus Christ, our Lord.

My prayer is that this book has helped all of you in some sort of way and that if you didn't know it before that you now know that there is freedom in Jesus and that you can have it. Even if it's not you personally who needs it, perhaps it's someone that you may know. You can share this story, my journey with them, to help them achieve freedom in Christ.

All of Heaven will be rejoicing when even just one person comes to The Lord. We must understand that we are our brothers and our sisters' keeper. If what I have to go through is hard and painful but it saves someone else, it brings them closer to The Lord and it leads them to be delivered and set free in Christ, then Lord, send me, I'll go. What I'm basically saying is, I understand that God created me. He created us all to help build His Kingdom, to love Him, and to love His people. One of the ways we love His people is by leading them to Christ. He told Peter, His disciple, "If you love me then feed my sheep." I hope that this book was fulfilling in some way for you.

I am so grateful for the opportunity to share my story with you all and, I'm grateful that God saw fit to use me as a vessel for honor and to do His good work. I actually used to serve in the women's ministry in my church. I led a group called, "Vessels for Honor." In this group, we would do a Bible study for six months teaching women and girls about who establishes their worth, how much our Heavenly Father loves them, teaching them about their relationship with Him and how to have meaningful, Godly relationships with others. The group was aligned with the scripture in 2 Timothy 2:21, "Those who cleanse themselves from the latter will be instruments for special purposes, made holy, useful to the Master and prepared to do any good work." At the end of the six months, there was a fashion show. Everyone would get dressed up in the most amazingly beautiful garments to give an outward expression of the inward transformation that had taken place. It was truly incredible to see the work that God had done. The life that He'd saved and changed to be used for His good works.

This book is for me- it's my fashion show, my debut. It's an outward expression of the inward transformation that has taken place on the inside of me. He is using me to do His good work and for this, I'm truly, truly grateful. I thank my God and I thank you from the very bottom of my heart. I strongly encourage you to go out and live a life free in Christ Jesus. Allow Him to use you. I promise you this, you won't regret it. Then share your freedom with someone else. You were created for this very reason. May God bless you and keep you and set you free. I love you!

Chapter Reflection:

"Allow Him to use you. I promise youthis, you won't regret it. Then share your freedom withsomeone else. You were created for this very reason. May God bless you and keep you and set you free."

Read and Meditate:

Psalms 107:1

Colossians 4:7

1 Thessalonians 5:16-18

Acknowledgements

Friends this has been a long-time-coming and a true labor of love. God told me that I was going to write books back when I was a young girl. Of course, I had no idea what I'd be writing about or who my audience would be. But I would definitely write. Honestly, I thought that I would have written more books by now but God's timing is always best. I now know that God was working on this particular book all this time. He was carefully knitting and weaving this book that would be perfectly placed in my womb and after much laboring, I've finally given birth to this beautiful book filled with purpose and promise.

My mama used to say all the time, "If I had ten thousand tongues, I could not begin to thank you enough, Jesus." Those are exactly my sentiments at this very moment.

None of this could have been possible without my Savior Jesus Christ. Jesus, you are my everything. I will forever love you and worship you and be a vessel of honor used by you to do your great work. Thank you, Toda Roda. Secondly, I thank my amazing husband, Daniel. Your boundless love and support have been the anchor that has sustained our family. I cannot thank God enough for bringing the two of us together. You are my forever love and my life partner. I'm so glad that I get to do life with you.

Then there are the Wandah babies, my children, Todd, Cody, Iffy, and Luca. I am the mother I am today because of all of you. I can't even begin to tell you how much I love you and how much I learn from all of you all the time. I am so honored that God chose me to be your mother and I wouldn't change one thing, not a single moment.

To Leslie Arroyo and Elder Marvin Kelly, my mentors, and spiritual advisors. Thank you for praying for me and with me and for holding me accountable and for always pointing me to Jesus.

Next, I'd like to thank my pastors, Shaun and Diana Nepstad, and my Fellowship Church family. You all are like no other. You asked me and my family to give you a year and you assured us that our lives would not be the same. Thank you for making good on that promise and for helping me to rediscover my purpose.

To Dr. Sherrie, Dr. Chris Walton, and Walton Publishing House, you are so much more than publishers. You are geniuses, God-breathed, spirit-filled, and divinely gifted individuals. Thank you for your creativity, your support, your patience, and your love for God and His creation. We did it! Thank you so much! Can't wait to do it again, lol!

Of course, I cannot go without saying thank you to my sister-friends. You are more than my friends, ladies you are like sisters to me. I hold a special place in my heart for each of you individually and collectively. You are the flowers in my garden and the pebbles in my pond and I love, love, love you so much. Thank you so much for the amazing and heartfelt quotes you provided for the book chapters.

Lastly, I have to give a Heavenly hug and thank you to my mama and daddy. I am because of you and so I thank you for my life, for all the love you gave, the lessons and the blessing, the gift of Jesus. You introduced me to Jesus when I was a very young girl and I've been riding with Him since. He's always been there. He's with me now. Thank you! Thank you! Thank you!

If there was anyone that I did not list here, please know that your names and faces are in my heart and I'm grateful for everyone that I've encountered. You are all a part of my story and I love you.

To reach Wandah for book signings and speaking engagements visit:

www.wandahparenti.com

www.ingramcontent.com/pod-product-compliance
Lightning Source LLC
Chambersburg PA
CBHW061203070526
44579CB00010B/116